An Angel a Day

The daily magic and inspiration of angels

MARGARET NEYLON

Element
An Imprint of HarperCollins*Publishers*
77–85 Fulham Palace Road
Hammersmith, London W6 8JB

The website address is:
www. thorsonselement.com

and *Element* are trademarks of
HarperCollins*Publishers* Limited

Published by Element 2003

1 3 5 7 9 10 8 6 4 2

A catalogue record of this book
is available from the British Library

ISBN 0 00 716513 7

Text illustrations by © John Spencer

Printed and bound in Great Britain by
Martins the Printers Limited, Berwick upon Tweed

Introduction

Angels are found all over the world, for they do not recognize boundaries of countries, language, creed or race. Angels are 'messengers from God', and they are in your life whether you follow a religion or not, and even if you don't believe in them! They are here to help and all we need to do is invite them into our lives, to point us in the right direction, so we can lead happy and abundant lives.

An Angel a Day offers a host of information to help you enjoy the angelic dimension in your life, including simple rituals, enjoyable tasks, fascinating quotations and inspirational messages to brighten each day. Make an Angel Shrine in your garden or home, plant flowers and shrubs the angels will enjoy, bake angel recipes for you and your loved ones, celebrate your angel's presence in many different ways. You can even invite the angels of each month and of the 12 zodiac signs into your life and see how easily things fall into place when you're doing the right thing at the right time!

You can follow this book through the year or simply dive in when you need angelic help. By connecting with angels every day of the year we become more aware of them and of the power we hold within our own hands to transform.

The angels can also help us live in harmony with all that our planet offers us. The better we treat our individual patch the better the planet will respond to us. I firmly believe that by aiding these 'beings of light' every day we can slowly yet surely bring the energy of angelic love closer and more clearly into every area of our lives and of our world.

I hope you enjoy this book and your angel daily!

Margaret Neylon

Welcome to An Angel a Day ...

If you have read my earlier books *Angel Magic* and *Open Your Heart to Angel Love*, you'll know that all the major religions mention angels in their holy scripture. This confirms that angels were created by God, while religions were created by mankind, and their presence has been passed on to us for thousands of years through stories, legends, ceremonies and rituals.

From ancient records we know that supernatural, winged creatures existed in the time of Mesopotamia and Sumeria, and in Greece and Rome. In Persia and India, people connected with *devas* (the 'shining ones'), which were then introduced into Judaism and Christianity as 'angels', and later into Islam, where they are known as *malaika*. Whatever their name, they are messengers from God who collaborate with humans and the other beings on the planet in order to bring harmony and co-operation into our world.

During the 7th century AD Pope Gregory the Great proclaimed there are nine 'orders of angels': angels, archangels, principalities, powers, virtues, dominations (dominions), thrones, cherubim and seraphim. The archangels, guardian angels and princes (principalities) are apparently the angels which connect directly with people and look after our planet. Personally I trust that the right angel will be with me when I am in need!

The Four Archangels

Archangels are mentioned in many Christian, Islamic and Jewish holy books, especially the Bible and the Koran, as well as in the Kabbalah. I see the archangels as the 'overseers' of the planet and all that happens here, while guardian angels are 'supervisors' in charge of giving us direction! If it was a business, I would imagine God as the chairman, the archangels as management, and the guardian angels as the workers, while humans would take on the role of their 'clients'!

Because the archangels relate to so many belief systems, here is some interesting information concerning each one.

Archangel Gabriel

Known as 'man of God' or 'God is my strength', Gabriel is the archangel of creativity and the arts, and looks after the zodiac signs Cancer, Scorpio and Pisces. Gabriel's task is to bring hope, justice, creativity and intuition to the greater consciousness of mankind.

Archangel Uriel

Uriel looks after the Planet Earth and all who inhabit it as well as the zodiac signs Gemini, Libra and Aquarius. It is Uriel's task to ensure constant, cyclical change in our planet and our lives, and to bring about universal cosmic consciousness.

Archangel Michael

Michael is also known as 'Who is like God' and is here to defend the weak and protect us. He looks after the zodiac signs Taurus, Virgo and Capricorn. Michael brings us patience, motivation, ambition and protection as we move forward to personal empowerment.

Archangel Raphael

Raphael (or Ramiel) means 'God has healed'. He looks after the fire signs Aries, Leo and Sagittarius. Raphael is the archangel in charge of the physical body, healing, health and longevity. His task is to bring love, joy, light and knowledge into our lives, including the current universal interest in angelic healing.

 4

About This Book

This book is to help you invite angels into your life and so make it rich and more colourful! You will see that each month is allotted an angel who looks after it, as is each astrological Sun sign. By connecting with them we enjoy their help and guidance to move more easily through the changing months and seasons.

Most of the 'Angel Inspirations' in the book are messages I received myself. I did not always understand their meaning but I began to use them – and quotations from books such as the Bible – in my 'Talking with Angels' workshops. I have added a short message under these 'inspirations' but you might also like to consider what these may mean to you personally.

This book is written initially for readers in the Northern Hemisphere, but I have also included some information for those living in the Southern Hemisphere.

The Angel of January

Gabriel

(Southern Hemisphere - Gabriel is the Angel of July)

Although this is only the start of the new calendar year (your own year begins on the day of your birthday), what better time to ask for insight into new opportunities awaiting us? A healthy introspection is one gift we can receive from Archangel Gabriel, the Angel of January, who brings us wisdom during the long, dark nights of winter.

Welcome Gabriel into your life by lighting a white candle (or night-light). Ensuring it is in a safe place, let the candle burn itself out and, as it does so, be aware that you are now at the beginning of a new era in your life. Everything that happened yesterday is now history, for today is always a new day. Focus on the candle flame and let its light inspire you. Perhaps it will shed some light on some areas of your life you have been ignoring, or give you the inspiration you need to start afresh. Remember that Gabriel is with you throughout the month of January to give you new vision.

Get the calendar year off to a good start by getting into a daily habit of inviting your angel to be with you at all times. A simple way to ensure angelic help every day in your life is to wake up and say the following before you even get out of bed. Say it aloud when you can, remembering the magic of the spoken word:

> *'The Angel of Divine Love goes before me*
> *and prepares my way.'*

If you start to say that on a daily basis then you will understand that whatever happens to you is meant to happen, it has been planned that way so that you can respond to it in your own way and learn from the experience.

*Not to believe in the angels is to believe in
a mindless, meaningless, and soulless universe.*

HAROLD BEGBIE, *ON THE SIDE OF THE ANGELS*

Is a belief in angels just a 'security blanket' to help us get through a bad day, or do they really exist? As I mentioned in the Introduction, angels have existed for thousands of years. All major religions acknowledge them. They are not 'New Age' beings, they are as old as God for they are God's messengers, not just beings of our imagination.

Do you know someone whose life seems meaningless just now? What about sending that person a little angel gift: perhaps an angel pin brooch, an angel bookmark or a card with an angel on it? These little things can mean such a lot, especially when life looks dull and grey.

4 January

Start an Angel Journal today. Invest a little money in a special book which can fit into your pocket or purse so that you can carry it around with you. Jot down all the special things that happen to you by 'synchronicity', which is what we often think is merely 'co-incidence', but is really the angels synchronizing events in order to get us to do the right thing at the right time. Keep this Angel Journal with you all through the coming year.

Everything in the Universe has an angel watching over it, including crystals, and their energy enhances our lives with balance, health and love. The more we become aware of how everything in the Universe can become a holistic part of our lives, the more 'whole' we will be. Those born in January especially should seek out a garnet, the crystal of this month. Garnet helps those suffering from anaemia and strengthens the heart, thyroid, liver and kidneys. It also helps to balance the sex drive, while bringing warmth and co-operation to interpersonal relationships. Together, garnet crystals and the angels can bring instant inspiration to tired minds!

Crystals can be worn as jewellery, carried in a pocket or kept in a special place in the home or workplace. It is important that you 'cleanse' your crystals as they pick up both negative and positive energy. The easiest way to do this is to leave them out of doors for a few nights at the time of the Full Moon, or outside in the sunshine on a bright, sunny day. You may also leave them overnight in a covering of sea salt, then gently wash it away under running water.

This is officially the end of the Christmas season. As you put away your decorations and dispose of your winter greenery for another year, thank the angels for being with you in your home over this period. Be aware that the devas, the Angels of Nature, who look after your garden throughout the year, are now returning to the outdoors after their brief respite in your home.

Light a candle to honour the help the devas give you each year as the seasons change, bringing growth, harvest and death as each cycle unfolds naturally.

By today most people will be back to work after the Christmas and New Year break. If you'd like to bring about some positive changes in your workplace do the following ritual:

Make a list of the people with whom you work or deal with during the working week. Remember each of those people has an angel (though it might be difficult to believe sometimes!). What you need to do now is write a letter to each of those people's angels, asking for harmony and companionship between you all in the workplace. If you'd prefer, you can simply write a general letter beginning with *'Dear co-workers' angels ...'* Enjoy the change in atmosphere as people become more willing to work together rather than against each other.

8 January

Know only that you are loved.

ANGEL INSPIRATION

To enjoy angelic presence in our own lives we do not need to be perfect or even try to be perfect. Angels offer 'unconditional love' – they set no rules, no standards to be fulfilled. Angels are here for us this instant, loving and guiding, giving us the support we need to move onwards and upwards towards spiritual enlightenment.

The only block to our happiness is our own fear, which is based on a belief that we do not deserve love. Love is the opposite of fear, and when we open to love we empty our hearts and minds of fear. When you are alone today, look into your eyes in a mirror and say aloud your name and *'I love you.'* See how you respond to this statement.

The start of the calendar New Year brings to mind how many things change within a given period. Each of us will have to face the loss of a loved one at some stage in our lives, and we will all react differently to that grief.

Sometimes we need the gentle care of a female angel, who can help us cope with grief and loss. Spend some time alone today remembering a loved one.

If you wish, light a blue candle in their memory. Remember, in particular, the joy and love you shared. When you need to express your grief, allow the comforting strength of your angel's wings to enfold you and keep you secure in the knowledge that you are loved.

10 January

Be an angel today! Practise a 'random act of kindness'. No-one else need know what you do, but the result will definitely be felt by someone. It may just be picking up litter. It may be offering to mind a child. Or even carrying away a Christmas tree to a recycling depot. Decide for yourself what you can do to be an angel today!

Whenever you want to connect with your angels, say the following words. They will help you to relax and connect with the best possible intentions in your mind:

'Angels of love, beings of light, please bring
enlightenment to me here and now.

Help me to bring magic into my life so that
I can share it with others.

Help me to fill my heart with love so that I can
share it with others.

Fill my heart with light and love as I speak to you now.'

12 January

Adopt a plant today!

Even though most of the trees, shrubs and flowers are dormant at this time, they do still need care and attention. Whether you own a pot plant or a large garden, or you simply walk in the local park, look about you today and see if there is any plant that needs extra care and attention. The Sufis of Islam believe that it takes seven angels to create a single leaf on a tree. Remember everything that grows has an angel looking after it, so give it a hand!

Perhaps your chosen plant needs to be sheltered from harsh January weather, or staked securely against the wind? Perhaps some weeds are strangling its growth? If you don't feel you can physically look after the plant, at least talk to it. You can do so simply by transferring kind, considerate thoughts into its energy field. From today converse with the plant and its angel on a daily basis if possible. Before long you'll see it blooming under your care.

Studies have shown that only those people who have a long-term focus for their future achieve life-long success. Do you drift along from day to day, or do you have a goal?

Now, at the beginning of the calendar year, it's time to focus on the future. This is the moment that you create it. Ask your angel to help you to find silence so that you can begin to create a wonderful outcome. Don't worry about the nitty-gritty, the angels will look after that for you, you just need to focus on the overall outcome. Just relax your body, then your mind, and imagine, deep within you, a spring of joy welling upwards. Feel the joy spreading outwards inside you. Let that joy fill every cell of your body. Let it flow through your limbs and out through your hands and feet. Let it fill your mind and cascade out of the top of your head and create an energy field of joy around you. Smile, laugh, giggle! Let joy be created and let it flow around you. You have now created a 'blueprint' for joyfulness as your long-term goal.

14 January

Outside the open window
The morning air is all awash with angels.

RICHARD WILBUR

No matter how gloomy it might seem outside, remember each day is a new day. Ask your angel to help you to remember this on awakening and, when you open your eyes, say aloud *'Today is a new day. I am a new me.'* With that knowledge firmly inscribed in your heart, every day can be a wonderful adventure!

Look at your talents. Make a list of them. Yes, make a list of all of them, whether it's budgeting your income, bringing up children so they can achieve their highest aims, cheering someone up with a bright, friendly smile or designing software to send rockets into outer space. Are you using your talents to your advantage or are you hiding them away? Are you proud of your achievements or are you unaware of them?

Each of us is unique, and we're meant to be unique. Not one of us is a clone of anyone else. Ask your angel to help you recognize your own uniqueness. Ask for help to shine as yourself. Celebrate your unique talents and skills. Share them with others and encourage others to shine in their own unique way, too.

*Those who walk with angels learn to soar
above the clouds.*

ANGEL INSPIRATION

Yes, even in the most well ordered life there will be clouds. The good news is that you're not alone when you need to face them. Respond to your angel's wish to connect with you. Get into the habit of starting the day by saying 'hi' to your angelic friend. Ask for help and you will receive it. Then you will find that you are soaring above the clouds of indecision and confusion, and you will discover the sky is always brilliant and blue.

Snowdrops are the traditional flowers of January. Have you seen any so far?

No matter what the weather, try to get out of doors today and search for those tiny, courageous little flowers, the first of the year. Just imagine being under the soil, dormant, for so long. Imagine the urge to waken and grow upwards, towards the warmth of the light, just as a snowdrop does. We, too, are similar. We need to wake up from a dormant time and move towards the light. That's how our angels can help us, they can point us in the direction of light. Ask your angel to do so today.

18 January

Teacher says every time a bell rings,
an angel gets his wings.

ZU ZU IN FRANK CAPRA'S *IT'S A WONDERFUL LIFE*

Take out a video of the Frank Capra film *It's a Wonderful Life* starring James Stewart. Consider the story behind it. We all make mistakes, after all, we're human! But we do have a reason for being here on the Planet Earth, and everything we do has a bearing on someone else, on some other outcome. Never give up, never despair! Your angel is always close by, willing to gently place its hand under your elbow and lead you forward.

19 January

Today is a day for saying 'thank you'. Start off by saying 'thank you' to your angel for all the love, care and protection you have enjoyed every moment of every day. Angels don't need to be thanked, but it's always nice to be on the receiving end of gratitude.

Now spend some time today going back through all the small gifts you've been given in recent weeks – the gift of a smile, an introduction, or even an unexpected present. Perhaps there are some people you forgot to thank. Just choose one or two people who have made a difference in your life and write them a 'thank you' card. It would be even more special if you made up your own greeting card. Ask Archangel Gabriel for some creative inspiration!

20 January

The Sun moves into the astrological sign of Aquarius today where it will stay for the next four weeks. Archangel Uriel looks after this Air sign of 'the water bearer', fulfilling the need to bring the flow of knowledge to the world.

Whatever your astrological sign, welcome Archangel Uriel into the world today, and wear the colours violet, white or indigo to attract its energy. Burn a blue candle to invite Archangel Uriel to be part of your life for the next month. Uriel looks after humanitarian concerns, which includes every being on the Planet Earth. Be very aware that everything you do will have an impact on our beautiful planet. Treat her kindly and with respect and we can all then share the benefits of her wonderful gifts.

If you are an Aquarian, be especially aware of Uriel in your surroundings for the next month. Are you fulfilling your path, that of 'bringing the flow of knowledge to the world'? How can you be even more aware and more proactive in this regard? Simply ask your angel!

May your neighbours respect you,
Trouble neglect you,
The angels protect you,
And heaven accept you.

IRISH SAYING

In an age where we can get virtually anything and everything that we want, it's important to understand and denote our priorities. While it's great to have a beautiful home, a comfortable car and a nice income, these things alone cannot make us feel fulfilled. Contentment comes from knowing that what is important to us is in our life. Good health, friendship and peace of mind cannot be bought, yet they are our prized possessions.

Today spend some moments thinking about the things in your life for which you are grateful: friendship, loving support, financial income, health ... Write out a list and finish it with a short but heartfelt *'Thank you, angels!'*

22 January

Go outside today and look at the changes in nature. Can you find a snowdrop? Can you see an aconite, or a crocus? How gentle and vulnerable these little flowers seem, yet they have battled the snow and the frost and survived the long winter.

When you see these little flowers pushing upwards towards the Sun, remember to give thanks to the devas, the Angels of Nature, who have nourished and encouraged them to grow. Say a big *'Thank you!'* to them for bringing life and beauty back into our world.

23 January

Do you ever talk to your Kitchen Angel? Yes, you do have one! If you find everyone seems to gravitate to your kitchen it's because your visitors are aware of it, most likely unwittingly.

Be extra aware of your Kitchen Angel today. Clean up any mess and try not to leave clutter around. Perhaps you would like to leave a special angel figurine or an angel magnet in this room to remind you of its presence. What about leaving a special place available for it? Make sure this space is tidy and comfortable, and remember to talk to your Kitchen Angel as often as possible. (You can just think words, you don't have to speak them aloud unless you wish to do so.) You just might be amazed at how your culinary skills begin to improve with the help of this nurturing angel.

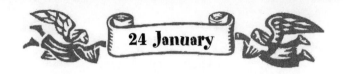

24 January

Angels speak to those who silence their
minds long enough to hear.

ANGEL INSPIRATION

In today's society it's so difficult to find silence. Yet if we do
not afford ourselves the gift of silence we shall never hear the
messages of our angels. Today spend five minutes in silence.
Empty your mind of anxieties and let the angels guide you in
what to say or, in fact, when to stay silent!

In Nordic cultures this is the day to celebrate 'The Disting Moon', when it is believed that whatever the weather is today will be repeated throughout the coming summer. First thing on waking today, invite the following angels into your environment and light a candle for each of them:

the Angel of the Sun,
the Angel of Water,
the Angel of Air,
the Angel of Earth.

(If you have the time, perhaps you would like to draw a picture showing the four of these elements in order to bring them more obviously into your life.)

Now ask these four angels to come together in perfect harmony over the coming months so that the summer can be a rich mix of rain and shine, light breezes to blow away any clouds, and a healthy, vibrant soil bringing forth healthy growth and nourishment.

No matter how strongly you believe in angels and their ability and willingness to protect you, there's no point in leaving the keys in your car with the door open in a place which is known for its amount of car theft! Each of us adults is responsible for taking care of ourselves and our belongings. Once we ask the angels to help protect us we can be certain they will. Do the following ritual to ensure your home is under angelic protection. (You can even expand it to your neighbours' property.) You don't even have to be physically present at your home when you do this.

Imagine you're getting a bird's eye view of your home, your garden, the footpath, your neighbours on either side ... See it in as much clear detail as possible.

Now imagine you see a funnel of bright light coming down from the heavens and it's covering the entire scenario. This is the light of angelic protection and, no matter what's happening in other areas around you, this section of your neighbourhood is now protected. It really is as simple as that!

*Be still. Quieten your mind. Know that I am
here with you.*
ANGEL INSPIRATION

It can be so difficult to believe and have faith that our angels
are here with us, willing us to do what we should do, know
what we need to know and share unconditional love between
us all. When times are tough our anxious mind often takes
over, chiding us for believing in angels, for believing in goodness, for believing in love.

By starting each day with two or three minutes of absolute
quiet during which we can connect with our inner self and
our angelic guidance, we can soon find ourselves on the right
path, doing the right thing. From today, set your alarm clock
to wake you up five minutes earlier than the norm. Use those
precious minutes to be still, quieten your mind and open up
to your angel's gentle love.

Have fun today making some Gingerbread Angels. Buy pastry cutters in the shape of angels, or else use a small triangular and circular pastry cutter. Alternatively, I have included here some templates of angels which you can use today, and also in other exercises throughout this book. Draw the templates at the desired size onto greaseproof paper and using a knife, gently run its blade over the tracing to form the Gingerbread Angels.

For about 20 small Gingerbread Angels, you will need:

125 g/4 oz margarine

175 g/6 oz sugar

275 g/9 oz treacle (molasses)

350 g/12 oz self-raising flour

1 medium egg, beaten

1 teaspoon baking soda

1½ teaspoons ground cinnamon

1½ teaspoons ground ginger

pinch of salt

chocolate chips, angelica or raisins, for decoration

In a saucepan, gently heat the margarine, sugar and treacle (molasses), stirring until everything is melted. Allow to cool, and then add the beaten egg and mix well. In a separate bowl, sift the self-raising flour with the baking soda, cinnamon, ginger and a pinch of salt, then add to the saucepan. Stir well, then chill.

Pre-heat the oven to 175°C/350°F/Gas Mark 5. Roll out the mixture on a lightly floured board until approximately ½cm/¼inch thick. If using a triangle cutter, cut 60 triangles (making up two wings and body for 20 angels). Then, using the circle cutter, cut 20 circles for the heads. Place these on a lightly greased baking. Decorate with chocolate chips, angelica or raisins to make angel faces. Bake for 10 minutes. Cool on a rack before serving.

Love is the highest form of attunement.

EDGAR CAYCE

We search and search for love and happiness and joy. We shall never find them outside of ourselves no matter how rich we become, no matter how old we become.

Unconditional love is what love, happiness and joy stem from. A flower cannot bloom without its bulb or seed. The growth and beauty start within that bulb or seed.

In our own lives it is the same. If we wish to attune with our angels and spiritual helpers, we must first learn to love ourselves unconditionally. Only then can we begin to love others unconditionally. Forgive yourself for not being perfect. Look in a mirror deep into your eyes and say aloud *'I forgive you.'*

Light a white candle today to thank Gabriel, the Angel of January, for looking after us during the month of January. Though this month can feel never-ending with little to show for it, do remember a lot of work is going on beneath the soil. We are just like the tiny bulbs pushing upwards from the dark, cold earth towards sunlight, facing difficult lessons on our own pathway to 'enlightenment'. Gabriel has been nurturing us through the long, dark nights and we can now release him as we move towards the brighter days of the year.

31 January

Today we welcome the Celtic Angel of the East into our lives. In Celtic lore this is the beginning of the festival of Imbolc, a special time celebrating birth, the female creative cycle and new milk. As the pastoral year is reborn with the soil warming up and the birth of new lambs, we need to pay tribute to Mother Earth for all she gives us, and to acknowledge the help of the devas, the Angels of Nature.

As the Sun sets tonight welcome the Angel of the East into the Northern Hemisphere. (In the Southern Hemisphere you will be celebrating Lughnasa, see 31 July.) As dusk approaches, surround yourself with lighted candles to welcome extra enlightenment into our lives at this time. Close your eyes and imagine you are a small shoot growing upwards through the soil and preparing yourself to burst free out into the brightness of the coming day. Feel the joy and sense of freedom that this brings! Thank the devas and Mother Earth for all they bring to us.

The Angel of February

Barchiel

(Southern Hemisphere - Barchiel is the Angel of August)

February is known as 'fill the ditch' time because of its rain and snow. Though we know that spring is on the horizon, we can lose faith easily during this month if we have to face harsh elements. Barchiel, the Angel of February, brings us light in the darkness and the gift of patience as we await a new dawning of growth.

Welcome Barchiel into your life by lighting a blue candle (or night-light) and, ensuring it is placed safely, allow it to burn itself out. As you watch the light burn, concentrate on the energies around the throat area, which is about communicating with integrity to others. Barchiel is with you now to help you to speak your truth during this month.

2 February

Traditionally this is a time for cleansing and purification. As you wash or shower yourself, say *'The Angel of Divine Light is now cleansing and purifying me.'* Collect your crystals and place them in a bowl of sea salt or else leave them outside in order for the Moon or the Sun to cleanse and re-energize them. If you have any angel figurines today is the day to clean and wash them.

Still on the theme of cleaning, lavender essential oil is a wonderful antiseptic and just a few drops in warm water can act as an alternative to harsher cleaning agents. Not only that, but your home will smell sweet, fresh and be a perfect place for relaxation. If you don't much like housework, ask the angelic beings in your home to join you, and you can bring fun and laughter into your duties by simply dancing with the hoover and singing with the mop!

4 February

In Celtic lore the beginning of February is the official start of spring. Go outside today and spend some time looking for new growth. Perhaps you can find some primroses or violets pushing their way out of the soil, braving the elements. These are the traditional flowers of February. Go and search for some today! Remember that *'every blade of grass has an angel standing over it saying "Grow! Grow!"'* (The Talmud). Flowers blooming at this time of year symbolize how we, too, can blossom after a time of struggle. Thank that angel for bringing you the gift of this little flower into your life today.

5 February

Be attentive to your angel and listen to its voice.

ANGEL INSPIRATION

Often we're so confused and unsure of where we're going that our minds are just a whirl of questions and fearful answers. Today, take some time just for yourself. Stop what you are doing. Unplug the phone and turn off the mobile. Now ask your angel for help to show you the right road. Calm your mind. Treat your fearful voice as though it is a child. Be kind and gentle, but firm. Take a few minutes just calmly breathing in and out, in and out. Ask a question. Now focus more on your inner feelings, the response that you get from inside, rather than the words in your mind. That's how you can listen to your angel's voice.

Make a 'goodbye' list. In a special jotter write down a list of all the habits to which you want to say 'goodbye': the habit of smoking, always being late, excessive eating or drinking, victim-consciousness, and so on. Ask your angel to help you to look at this list with honesty and truth. Taking one item at a time, review how this has affected your life. What do you gain from it? What do you lose? When you feel you understand why you have been following that habit, say 'thank you and goodbye' and cross it off your list. Remember to call on your angel for help in this regard should you need it in the future.

Amethyst is the crystal for the month of February. It ranges in colour from deep pink to violet, which is the colour to attract Archangel Uriel, who governs Aquarians. The name comes from the Greek *amethystos* which means 'not drunk', as this stone apparently protects the wearer from the negative effects of alcohol! Amethyst also strengthens the immune system and the endocrine system, cleansing the blood and pineal glands. Purchase an amethyst crystal today if you don't already own one, and cleanse it either by the Sun or Moon's rays, or in sea salt. Whenever you look at it or touch it, bring into mind Archangel Uriel who is currently overseeing this zodiac sign of Aquarius.

Clear out one room of your home. If you cannot spare the time to clear the entire room just begin with one cupboard or one drawer. As we clear our own space of unnecessary clutter we are unconsciously giving ourselves permission to clear out used emotions, hidden hurts, blame and shame. Don't take the entire house on today, just start to clear things out of your life slowly but surely over the coming weeks. As we give ourselves more physical space, we also give ourselves space to speak our own truth with integrity and love.

9 February

I want to be an angel
And with the angels stand –
A crown upon my forehead
A harp within my hand.

URANIA LOCKE BAILEY

What must it be like to be an angel, a 'being of light'? How wonderful it must feel to be free of the physical body that we humans all have and fly at a moment's notice, and at a millisecond's speed, to different places upon this planet! Imagine what it is like to be an angel! Close your eyes and imagine you are above this building, high up in the blue sky. Look down and notice what is beneath you. Now you can see your life as though it is a tapestry, showing which way to turn, which roadway to follow. For just a few moments, free yourself today from the cares that hold you a prisoner and sing with joy!

10 February

Encourage the warmth of the Sun to waken the garden and so begin the cycle of new life. Massage a yellow candle with an essential oil such as neroli or lemongrass and then light it. As you watch the candle burn, concentrate on the flame for a few moments which will help you to relax and distance yourself from any cares you have today. Close your eyes and imagine the devas, the Angels of Nature, dancing and humming in the garden, waking up the sleepy plants and bulbs. Watch how the garden begins to come alive again under their ministrations. Laugh with them.

Has someone ever acted 'like an angel' to you? Now is the time to show your thanks for his or her angelic deed. Why not make up a special card to show your appreciation for their love and support? St. Valentine is the symbol of love, so send your messages of thanks or love to that person who helped you 'like an angel'. Remember to post your card in good time!

12 February

When we use words either verbally or in writing we are literally making a spell. (The word 'spell' comes from the French word *espeler* which translates as 'to read out' or to 'name the letters of a word'.) As we move towards the universal day of love, why not weave a spell into a special handmade Valentine's card or a handmade gift for your beloved? As you think of this person, send loving thoughts and memories into the object you are making and say aloud, *'The Angel of Divine Love is now a part of this gift that I am making.'* You may be surprised at the change that comes about once this object has been handed over to your beloved.

Celebrate St. Valentine by baking these 'Little Cupids' tarts.
You will need:

For the shortcrust pastry

425 g/15 oz frozen pastry (thaw for 90 mins. Place on lightly floured surface before cutting)

or if you are making the pastry yourself:

165 g/6 oz plain flour

2 teaspoons sugar

½ teaspoon salt

120 g/4 oz butter or margarine

2–3 tablespoons water

For the filling and topping

125 g/4 oz macaroons

3 tablespoons sherry or brandy

150 ml/5 fl oz whipping cream

angelica or cherries, for decoration

Mix the flour, sugar and salt into a bowl, add the butter/margarine, and blend with fingers or in an electric blender until it resembles fine breadcrumbs. Add the water, gradually, to ensure the dough sticks together.

Roll out the dough on a floured surface to ½ cm/¼ inch thickness. If possible, use shell design baking trays, otherwise use ordinary bun baking trays and 'scallop' the rims of the pastry circles with a knife. Pre-heat the oven to 220°C/425°F/Gas Mark 7, and bake 'blind' for 15–20 minutes, then cool.

Break the macaroons into pieces, and then put them in the blender and reduce to fine breadcrumbs (or put them into a plastic bag and crush them with a rolling pin.) Add 3 tablespoons of sherry or brandy to the fine biscuit crumbs and leave to soak for a few minutes.

Whisk the cream until stiff. Stir in the crumb mixture and put it into the cooked tart shells. Top them off with angelica or cherries. Serve with love.

In Roman times men refused to go to war because they were more comfortable at home with their wives, hence marriage was banned! A religious man, Valentine, performed the marriage ceremony for loved ones in secret and was imprisoned, and later killed, because of his good deed. Those who appreciated his act sent him hearts and roses in thanks, and so St. Valentine's Day became a special day for lovers.

If you have a partner, celebrate your love today and ask the angels of both of you to help you to communicate your love and understanding throughout the year. Be thoughtful of those who are lonely and have recently lost love. Ask their angels to help them to open up to angelic love and so heal any wounds in their heart. If you count yourself as one of the latter, sit quietly with a lit candle in front of you and, closing your eyes, ask your angel to pour love into your heart.

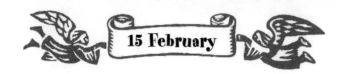

15 February

To attract love into your life, make up this special blend of naturally perfumed oil. Use a small dark-coloured bottle and add the following to a carrier oil (such as almond, olive or grapeseed oil):

> 3 drops rose or rosewood essential oil
>
> 3 drops sandalwood essential oil
>
> 3 drops ylang ylang or jasmine essential oil

Shake the bottle gently then dab some oil on your wrists, behind your ears, and so on. It can also be used in an oil burner.

16 February

These things, I warmly wish for you –
Someone to love, some work to do,
A bit of sun, a bit of cheer,
And a guardian angel always near.

IRISH SAYING

There's nothing so cheering on a winter's day as receiving a note from someone sending you warm wishes. Why not send this short message to someone you know today who could do with a little light relief? Go on, add some pictures or write it in beautiful calligraphy. It won't only cheer the sender up, it will make you feel good, too!

17 February

Look out for a robin in your surroundings today. In many ancient lores a robin symbolizes a messenger from heaven. Have you lost someone in recent months? Perhaps this robin could be the spirit of that person returning to say 'thank you' and brighten up your day with song and colour. If so, thank the robin for coming and bringing with it its angelic message.

18 February

Your angel is here to help you, so don't forget to ask it to connect you with someone special who you can trust before inviting them into your life. Then, if you want to create an intimate environment, fill your surroundings with the essence of love. Put a little carrier oil (such as almond, grapeseed or rose oil) and water in the 'well' of an aromatherapy oil burner, and then add the following mix of essences:

     2 drops patchouli essential oil

     2 drops orange or neroli essential oil

     2 drops cinnamon essential oil

(You might like to choose an oil burner in pink (for love) if possible.)

Today the Sun moves into the astrological sign of Pisces where it will remain for the next four weeks. Archangel Gabriel looks after this Water sign, its symbol being two fish tied together, each facing the opposite direction. Pisces is about personal freedom. We all tend to restrict ourselves through believing our own fears. Archangel Gabriel can help us to see that the only limitations we have are those we construct ourselves.

Welcome this archangel into your life today, no matter which sign you are. Wear the colours silver, white or blue to attract its energy to you.

Pisceans should be particularly aware of Archangel Gabriel in their lives for this four-week period. Ask for extra help to find focus in what you should be doing so that you can concentrate your energies in the right direction.

Beloved, let us love one another, for love is from God.

JOHN 4:7, THE BIBLE

What is life without love? Fear is only the opposite of love, and doesn't exist in reality. It is just a thought. Reach out today and respond in love instead of fear. You'll be surprised at the outcome!

Have you yet noticed how many songs include the word 'angel' within their lyrics? This is a very special word, meaning 'messenger from God', and if you stop and listen when the word occurs in songs it will help you be more aware of their presence on a daily basis. Make a game of counting up as many songs as you can which mention 'angel'. Then sing as many as you know. Share the fun with friends and children in your day and help them to move into more awareness, too.

In a dream, in a vision of the night when
deep sleep falls upon men slumbering
upon their bed, then God opens their ears
and seals in their instructions.
BOOK OF JOB 33:14–16, THE BIBLE

The sign of Pisces is ruled by the planet Neptune, which can help us connect deeply with our dreams. Angels often come to us in our dreams because we may be too fearful to open up to them in daylight! Get into the habit of asking your angel for a helpful dream before you go to sleep. Remember that all dream images are symbols. Record what you saw. What do those symbols mean to you?

As I mentioned earlier, Pisces is a Water sign, and this element often runs out of control and spreads over too wide a canvas. It's vital that you focus on what you want to do, rather than divide your energy into too many areas, seeking to fulfil too many demands. Light a silver, white or blue candle today and ask Archangel Gabriel to help you focus on what is important to you, and give you the patience to see it through.

When I fly I think of three things:
faith, hope and gravity.

MILTON BERLE

Angels have a sense of humour. We need to remember that or we can easily get bogged down in taking ourselves too seriously. During today, take some time to think of the things that are foremost in your mind. It's important to understand that each of us does have a purpose in life and we do need to follow our path, but we must also get things into proportion. The angels want us to enjoy our lives. That's why they're here to help us. Have a good laugh at yourself every now and again for taking life too seriously. Then take time to laugh with the angels!

25 February

Though it may be cold and blustery outside, you can create an indoor Angel Shrine somewhere in your home. It doesn't have to take up a large space; just a small space on a bookshelf is fine if that's all you can spare.

Put something special there to remind you of your angel. Perhaps a figurine or a picture or card depicting an angel. Over the days collect special items to place there. Remember this is to honour your angel, so anything that reminds you of its presence in your life should go here. Perhaps you'd like to place a white feather or a have a vase with a flower in it. You can also place any problem you have here and let your angel look after it for you, i.e., a bill, an angry letter, the name of someone with whom you are arguing, and so on. Trust that your angel is now working on this situation for you in the perfect way.

It's the beginning of spring and we need to break free of the restrictions of winter. The days are longer and brighter, new growth is all around us. Greet the day as the Sun rises above the horizon. Be very aware that everything that has energy is a living entity. Go out today as early as possible into the fresh spring air. Spend time in your garden, in a park, or in the country. Be aware of the soil warming up, of the growing bulbs and plants around you. Remember also to greet the devas, the Angels of Nature, who are looking after all these living things!

Show hospitality to strangers for, by doing that,
some have entertained angels unawares.

HEBREWS 13:2, THE BIBLE

When we listen to the news or read the newspapers it's easy to become fearful of the unknown and, of course, those who are strangers. Yet it can often be the case that we can receive the very message we've been waiting for from a total stranger, someone who seems to 'appear out of nowhere' with the pertinent information. Yes, that person can be an angel, or a person who has been nudged by an angel to give you a message. Today, show hospitality to someone who is a stranger by simply smiling and saying 'hello', or attend a meeting where you will meet new contacts. Be open, be aware, and remember everyone has an angel.

28 February

Say thanks and goodbye to Barchiel, the Angel of February, today. It's 28 days since the start of February, so ask Angel Barchiel to help you see how far you've come in ridding yourself of the past and freeing yourself for the future. Is there anything you've overlooked? Light a blue candle and stare at its flame until you feel calm and relaxed. Then close your eyes, and breathe deeply. Take time for yourself to look into your heart and discover if there is anything more that you need to let go of.

Leap Year

This is an extra special day because it comes around only every four years. Celebrate this extra 24 hours which we have been given as though it is a special gift, which it is. Can you imagine how you would feel if you were given only one more day to live? What would you do? How would you fill those 1,440 minutes of those 24 hours? Light a blue or white candle and, closing your eyes, ask your angel to help you let go of any fears which are holding you back from accepting all the good which is your right. Remember that 'inexperience' does not mean 'inability'. Be willing to give things a chance without needing a guarantee of success.

The Angel of March

Machidiel

(Southern Hemisphere - Machidiel is the Angel of September)

At last the daylight is with us longer, and there's a sense of spring about! With the help of Machidiel, the Angel of March, we can enjoy a boost to our inner strength which will give us the courage to begin to sow the seeds that later in the year we will be harvesting. It is with this angel that we celebrate the Spring Equinox, the symbol of balance between the Sun and Moon (symbolizing fire of action and receptivity of intuition). Light a yellow or green candle to welcome Machidiel into your life today. The yellow denotes sunshine and optimism, the green verdant growth.

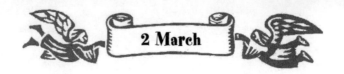

The soil is warming up and it's time to start seriously tending your garden. If you want to enjoy a full harvest you need to take into account the life of the earth, the effect of the elements and planets (especially the Moon), and, of course, the devas (the Angels of Nature) living in the garden. We get so much joy and contentment from our gardens that we must try to respect the energies there. If possible, have a patch which is just for wild flowers and, yes, weeds! Weeds are 'seeds gone to waste' yet they all have a reason for existing. They keep the ecosystem in balance by feeding the insects which feed the birds which spread the seeds which grow and enrich the soil. As you work, greet the devas who are working away, usually unseen, to create the beauty that surrounds us.

Look at the wonders around you!

ANGEL INSPIRATION

Today is about awakenings. Go for a walk and see what flowers have come into bloom. The anemone is the traditional flower for March. There could also be violets, daffodils, bluebells, wallflowers, lesser celandine ... Despite the wind, cold, rain and dark days of winter these tiny flowers have risen to greet the spring. Stop and look at these wonders around you. Then greet them and their angelic helpers by saying *'Hail be, unto thee, oh good living flower, made by the Creator!'*

Aquamarine is the crystal for the month of March. Those born within this month should endeavour to get one of these crystals, and it's also a good idea to attract its energies and healing properties into your life, no matter which month holds your birthday. Aquamarine means 'water from the sea' and is thought to protect people from irrational fears, and also helps to detoxify the human body. When you carry or wear this stone you are also attracting the angels of protection and health into your life. Hold one of these crystals in your hand and say aloud *'The Angel of Divine Protection goes before me and prepares my way.'*

When I first started my Angel Workshops and 'came out of the closet' about my belief in angelic beings, quite often people would not believe that they existed. I wouldn't push people to believe, but instead I would get the angels to act for me in simple ways and so prove their existence.

One sure way of discovering you have an angel is to ask it to help you find a parking space in a specific area, particularly if you need to find one in a built-up urban sprawl. It's simple, just ask your angel for *'a perfect parking space, thank you'*, preferably remembering to ask before you arrive at the required spot! You and your non-believing company will be amazed at how readily these 'worth a fortune in gold' parking spots manifest for you.

Gratitude unlocks the fullness of life. It turns what we
have into enough, and more. It turns denial into
acceptance, chaos to order, confusion to clarity.
It can turn a meal into a feast, a house into a
home, a stranger into a friend. Gratitude makes
sense of our past, brings peace for today, and
creates a vision for tomorrow.

MELODY BEATTIE

Angels don't need thanks, it's their job to help us. But it's good to show them gratitude for being with us through good times and bad. Learn to say *'Thank you, angels!'* no matter what the outcome.

Take time to meditate today. All you need is ten minutes of silence without distractions. Close the door. Turn off the phone. Get comfortable. Play music gently in the background if you like. Let your mind drift and tell yourself that no-one needs you right now, and you need do nothing right now. Breathe in deeply. Breathe out deeply. Imagine that your angel is now beside you, very close to you. What do you want to say to your angel? What do you want to receive? As your breathing deepens and steadies you will drift off into another space. Let whatever happens happen.

When you come back gently into your body you'll feel more relaxed and more vibrant. Write down any feeling, message, colour or object you may have seen or heard during your moments of peaceful connection. What do they mean to you?

Have fun today! The great thing about fun is that it doesn't have to cost you anything except the time that you give over to enjoying it! Whether you're alone or share your life with someone old or young, be spontaneous today. It's important to realize that fun isn't a waste of time, it's a method of creating healthy energies within you. Consciously invite your angel to spend the day with you: be like a child again, unquestioning and 'open to outcome'. Don't expect any result, just do something that's fun: have a skipping contest, go roller-skating, play hopscotch, make paper doilies, cut up old greeting cards and make a collage. It doesn't have to cost you anything to have the greatest day of your life!

It's time to check on your garden. Are weeds coming up where you want to grow something special? If so, spend time outside talking either aloud or in your mind to the weeds and the angels of the weeds (yes, they do have angels!). Ask that they make preparations to allow you to clear them from this particular place in the garden. Remember most weeds have medicinal properties, so don't destroy them all, just transplant them to another part if possible. If you then leave the garden overnight, you should find the weeds are much easier to pluck from the ground. Try it, it works!

If you want to tell anything to God, tell it to the wind.

AFRICAN PROVERB

God is everywhere. You don't have to wait till Sunday or the Sabbath to communicate. There's something very special about communing with nature and the elements. Don't draw the curtains and close the door on these gifts from God. Spend time in the open air today being part of this wonderful planet, rather than isolating yourself from it!

Try this delicious pasta dish: Angel Hair with Balsamic Tomatoes. For 2–3 servings you will need:

6 large tomatoes, chopped (or a 400 g/14 oz tin of tomatoes)

fresh basil, chopped (according to taste)

2 tablespoons balsamic vinegar

salt and pepper

2 garlic cloves, crushed

1 tablespoon olive oil

200–250 g/8–9 oz angel hair pasta

Place the chopped tomatoes, basil and balsamic vinegar in a bowl and season. Leave to stand for 10 minutes, stirring occasionally. In a frying pan, sauté the garlic in olive oil until lightly browned.

Cook the pasta in boiling salted water for 5–6 minutes. Drain the tomatoes, keeping the juice. Cook them gently with the garlic for 1–2 minutes. Toss the tomatoes and pasta together, sprinkle with the balsamic tomato juice and serve with Parmesan cheese.

12 March

Speak to a wise person today. It could be a stranger at a bus stop; it could be a spiritual counsellor, a teacher or a friend. Or it could be your angel. Write down any message you receive. Even if you don't immediately understand the words, guard them closely in your heart and mull over them at your leisure.

Do some work in your garden or with your potted plants. Even a tiny primrose or primula (the first rose of the spring) can brighten up a dull spot. And, remember, every flower has an angel looking after it. Greet that angel today!

Now is the time to hard-prune some plants, in particular angel's blush hydrangea (*Hydrangea paniculata 'ruby'*) which has lilac-like heads and will grow to be quite tall again, flowering in August and September. If you are growing the herb angelica, you need to move the seedlings now, rather than wait for the tap root to develop. Angelica has large, wide leaves and needs to be in a somewhat sheltered place with plenty of room to grow, and a mixture of sun and shade. It also needs plenty of water in order to flourish.

You are the Light Bearer. By sharing your increasing
knowledge you are enlightening others.

ANGEL INSPIRATION

Where did you first hear about angels? Who told you that you have this 'being of light' looking after you? Can you quantify the positive influence this has had for you? You, too, can enlighten others. You don't have to teach, you don't have to lecture, just mention your own angel to someone who is in need of extra help, or to someone who seems receptive. See yourself as someone moving through the darkness of loneliness and fear and bringing with you a bright light to obliterate dark corners of people's lives.

As we move towards the Spring Equinox, where day and night are of equal duration, we are preparing for new growth. What do you wish for in the coming months? Start to bring them about by making a prayer boat. All you need is a sheet of paper and a pen, then write out all the things you would like in your life right now. Don't worry, there's more than enough to go around, so ask for anything and everything. Now you can make this paper into a boat. Remember doing this as a child?

1. Fold paper in half.

2. Finding the middle of the folded part, fold down either side to form 'sails'.

3. You now have two sails at the top. At the bottom there are two open ends. Fold each of these separately outwards so that they form the hull beneath the sails.

4. Taking both ends of the boat, fold in two, so that it looks like a hat.

5. Make a small fold at each of the lower points of the 'hat'.

6. Holding each of these folds, pull them apart. This should now form a sailable vessel.

Now you can symbolically float that boat in your sink or your bath, or if you know you will not be causing pollution, send it on its way to the angels in a river, stream or ocean.

Be not afraid.

ANGEL INSPIRATION

Fear is only a thought, it is not a reality. The opposite of fear is love. Rub a candle with lavender essential oil, then sit down quietly, light the candle and open up your heart to love. Imagine the energy of love, perhaps seen in green or pink, coming into your heart. It's filling it up with every breath that you take. Now there's no room for fear any longer. Open your eyes onto a new world, one that is filled with love.

Make an Earth Shrine today. An Earth Shrine is a special place to honour the Angels of Nature, the devas. It can be as big or small as you wish, and if all you can achieve is a shrine in an indoor pot plant, that's fine. The point is that you create it with love and thankfulness. It's just a miniature garden but the special thing about it is that it's dedicated to the devas. Place it where it is sheltered and will not be disturbed. If you are lucky enough to have a large garden you could design it with a place for you to sit and meditate. Put an angel figurine in it, with crystals and stones that appeal to you. Use natural products where possible. You can change your Earth Shrine and add to it whenever you feel it is necessary so that there is something growing in it all year round.

Choose an area of your life where you are not happy, for instance, family or intimate relationships, your career or financial prospects. Now take a pen and paper and write out a brief history of how you usually respond to that area. Keep it simple. Go on for as long as you wish but in quite a short time you should see a pattern emerging that you were not aware of before. This pattern you've been following now needs to be changed.

If you wish to have a different outcome, you must change your usual pattern of behaviour. Ask Archangel Gabriel for inspiration and help if you find it difficult to change that pattern.

Adopt a tree today. Look around you in your neighbourhood. Is there a tree that looks as though it is struggling to survive? Are weeds choking its ability to grow? What can you do to help it thrive? Just a gentle touch with your hand (or even better, a hug) can help to transfer energy into its flagging spirits. Talk to the tree, talk to the devas in the surrounding area. Ask for extra special energy to be sent to this tree. Thank the tree for taking all the carbon dioxide we create and transforming it into oxygen in order for us to breathe and so live.

You, alone, are enough.

ANGEL INSPIRATION

To the world you might be just one person, but to one person you just might be their world! That's a lovely quote I picked up recently from someone's email. Think about it!

21 March

The Sun moves into the zodiac sign of Aries, a Fire sign, today. Archangel Raphael looks after this month. It's also the first day of the old new year, which began around the time of the Spring Equinox in the Northern Hemisphere, and also heralded the beginning of the pastoral growing season.

Today wear something yellow to encourage joy, enthusiasm and new growth into your life. Spend some time today asking Archangel Raphael to fill you with energy to bring new awareness into your own life. Light a yellow candle to celebrate this Archangel's presence in your life and in the world generally.

The Spring Equinox is celebrated today in the Northern Hemisphere. (If you live in the Southern Hemisphere you will be celebrating the Autumn Equinox.) Today the day and night are of equal measure and we are entering a period of brightness and verdant growth. Welcome personal growth into your life today with this visualization. Ensure you are sitting in a comfortable place without any distraction.

Breathe in deeply and, as you breathe out, allow yourself to drift away from the cares of the day. Just imagine now that your feet are reaching into the earth below you. There is nothing to fear, the soil is soft, warm and welcoming. You know you are rooted in it, perfectly safe, perfectly calm. Now as you breathe in you can feel the energy of the earth coming into you. It's as though you have a stem instead of a body and the energy is travelling upwards, making you feel refreshed and strong. Now the energy is moving into your limbs. You realize you are like a beautiful flower, growing tall and strong. Feel the energy move into your limbs, it's as though they have become soft, delicate petals. The energy is filling them with joy and love. You want to open up to joy and love, so you open up your petals.

It's wonderful being a flower! Feel the soft delicacy of the petals, the strength of your leaves and stem. Now you can feel a gentle raindrop land on one of your petals and you feel a sense of joy at its touch. The gentle breeze blows and you can feel yourself moving with the breeze, as though you're dancing. Everything around you is alive. Look around you. Feel how wonderful it is to be this flower.

Enjoy this feeling for some minutes then allow yourself to slowly return to the room and, breathing normally, bring yourself back into your body from your head all the way down to your feet.

What flower were you? What do you think this symbolizes in your life?

Listen, it's the voice of your angel!

ANGEL INSPIRATION

Sometimes we expect our angel to speak to us directly in its own voice. Yes, if you are clairaudient that can happen. However, angels often nudge ordinary human beings to say extraordinary things! If you're trying to connect with your angel and get a message, listen to other people's words, especially today. You could be in receipt of the exact answer you've been waiting for, but this time it comes from another person's lips.

Today is the festival of Archangel Gabriel. Gabriel looks after creativity and the arts. It is when we use our right brain that we can imagine all sorts of wonderful things which can then be manifested into reality. Whether it's painting a picture, writing a poem or making something with your own hands, Gabriel is always close by. We all need to use our right brain more.

Today spend time just imagining wonderful things happening or, even better, paint, draw, dance, make music or sing. Surround yourself with the colours of silver, white and/or blue. Light a candle specially in his name, and thank Archangel Gabriel for imbuing you with the creative spark on this, his special day.

Today is Lady Day, which is a day to thank Mother Nature for all her burgeoning gifts. Spend time looking after your Earth Shrine, go for a walk in a park or garden, or visit a garden centre if you have no garden of your own. Look at the astonishing array of flowers and plants on display. Really look at them: at the leaf, at the petal, at the colour, at the new buds. How amazing nature proves to be! Isn't it time you offered Mother Nature a gift? Leave a small crystal in thanks for all these gifts or, better still, take some 'crystal seeds', which are tiny crystals and cost very little, and spread them around the growing area.

You can never have too many flowers and plants in your life, whether indoors or outside. By filling your surroundings with growth you are inviting many angels and devas to share your life with you.

Today, why not get a variety of plant pots and paint angels on them. You don't have to be an artist to do so, your local hardware store, DIY or craft shop probably has angel stencils you can buy. If you can include children, family or friends in your activity you can arrange a 'Pot Party' and exchange different designs with each other. Make it fun and you can be sure your angels will be sharing the joy with you!

Archangel Raphael has many tasks and one is to look after the evening winds. If at all possible try to spend some time out of doors this evening. Dress suitably in order to be able to stand outside quietly for 15 minutes or so with your eyes closed. Do nothing but feel the evening breeze touching your face. Talk to Archangel Raphael, or your own angel, and ask to be made more aware of the elements around you.

Silence is the language of the angels.

ANGEL INSPIRATION

When you love someone it's difficult to let them go through their own 'learning curve' without attempting to force them into doing what you think is right. If you're currently in such a situation, ask your angel to help you to keep silent when necessary or to speak out when necessary.

If you, yourself, are going through your own 'learning curve' and desperate for help, you need to find silence in your life in order to connect with angelic guidance.

It is believed that orchids are the most highly evolved flowers in the entire plant world. Those who have studied them have found that their colour, form and scent contain amazing healing vibrations. Is it possible for you to grow an orchid either as a potted plant or in your garden? If so, watch as it grows and unfolds. Try to communicate with the orchid and its deva, especially if you need colour and magic in your life. Just speak aloud to them or else do so intuitively. If it's not possible to have a real orchid in your life, get a picture of one that you can hang up in an area of your home where you can see it every day to remind you of its healing power.

May you always have an angel by your side,
Watching out for you in all the things you do.

DOUGLAS PAGELS

Write out the message above on a small slip of paper. Add to it with different colours, sparkles or 'angel confetti' (which is available in the shops nowadays), if you wish. Carry it with you and, when you feel someone is in great need of an angel by their side, slip it into their hand or their bag or pocket. If you feel that may be intruding, however, leave it between the pages of a book in a library or bookshop. Don't worry, the angels will guide the right person to find their message.

31 March

This is the last day of the month and it's time to thank Machidiel, the Angel of March, for being with you at this time.

Look back through your Angel Journal that you began at the beginning of the year and see how Machidiel has helped you to find the balance between the Moon and the Sun, the power of intuitive understanding and the ability to put things into action.

The Angel of April

Asmodel

(Southern Hemisphere - Asmodel is the Angel of November)

1 April

April is a wonderful month, full of promise and expectation. It's a time of renewal and rebirth. Now that the Sun is shining and the days are longer we have the energy to try new things, meet new people, look to new horizons. All around us we can celebrate the gift of new life by inviting Asmodel, the Angel of April, to join us this month.

Get a white candle and surround it with flowers of the season. As it burns, imagine you see Angel Asmodel working with the flowers and plants outside in the gardens and fields. Think of how you can help improve your own environment and bring more beauty into your surroundings.

2 April

Maybe the tragedy of the human race was
that we had forgotten we were each Divine.

SHIRLEY MACLAINE, *OUT ON A LIMB*

Within each of us there is a tiny diamond, a connection to the Divine. This diamond has many facets. Some are brilliant, some give out a dull glow, some need to be polished. That's why we're here at this 'University of Life', to polish that diamond till every facet shines!

Diamond is the crystal dedicated to the month of April. Unless you can afford real diamonds, look out for clear quartz crystal which will help you see your current situation with more clarity than before.

In the old days when people were facing problems, they would be advised to 'sleep on it'. If you have any particular problem or uncertainty at the moment, place a clear quartz crystal under your pillow tonight and ask your angel to give you more understanding of the issue.

So often, without realizing it, we drift from day to day, week to week and, worse, year to year! Then we look back and wonder what happened to all those years. As we move into a new month we need to focus on what we want to achieve over the next four weeks. You don't need to know the exact steps to take; all you need is to know how you want to feel as you leave April behind.

Sit quietly, without interruption, and ask your angel and the angel Asmodel to be with you. Imagine there are tiny roots coming out of the soles of your feet and growing deep into the ground. These are keeping you firmly fixed and committed to your future success. Now create in your mind's eye feelings of joyfulness, excitement, enthusiasm and a sense of adventure. It's the feeling you need to develop here, that's all. All you need do is imagine a wonderful feeling as your outcome. When you have this firmly fixed in your heart you know you have sown the seeds for a wonderful outcome at the end of April.

Belief. You cannot buy it, for it doesn't come in a box all wrapped up in pretty paper. You cannot steal it or borrow it, and no-one can teach it to you. Yet still we believe. We believe in things we do not always see, things we cannot touch.

Belief is something that grows in us. No-one can stop us believing in angels once we've been touched by their presence. And yet we cannot prove they exist, except with hindsight, looking back over our lives and seeing how the angels have helped us.

It's important that you believe in you, too! Once your angel is by your side everything is possible. Acknowledge that now. Open up your heart to your angel and ask for extra help in believing in yourself. Then go and scale that mountain! When you look back, with hindsight, you'll wonder how you could ever have lacked belief in your own abilities.

Do not fear, greatly beloved, you are safe.

DANIEL 10:15, THE BIBLE

So said the angel to Daniel as he faced a life-threatening ordeal. We all have to face our fears, but when you know that you have an angel at your side, you will be safe. The angel's presence will help you see how fear is only a thought, and when we look at that thought we can vanquish it. Ask your angel to help you face your fears today.

Visit your Earth Shrine that you created in the middle of March. Make sure you weed it and tend and cultivate it. Is there anything missing? The daisy and the sweet pea are the flowers for April. Despite the fact that we often treat the daisy as a weed, it has healing qualities: chewing the fresh daisy leaf helps cure mouth ulcers, they taste good in salads, and an infusion can help respiratory tract problems and clear the skin. Perhaps you would like to plant some sweet peas in this Earth Shrine, and seedlings should be readily available at this time. Make sure you plant them in a place where they can climb upwards. Depending on space, you could make a 'teepee' of bamboo sticks, tied together at the top, up which the sweet peas can clamber and flourish.

Angel power is a free gift from God
available to everyone.
An Angel Insurance Policy will give you
a blessed hedge against the unforeseen.

JANICE T. CONNELL, *ANGEL POWER*

We shall all face difficult tasks on occasion. It's perfectly normal because we're here at this 'University of Life' to learn what we need to know, and sometimes those lessons can be painful. Wouldn't it be a relief to be able to claim extra help from your Angel Insurance Policy at times when you are most in need? You can! You can ask for extra angelic insurance today!   .

All you need to do is create a 'spell'. (As I mentioned before, this is simply putting things into words.) Get a pen and paper (it's more effective if you actually write it rather than type it), and write out your own Angel Insurance Policy, along the lines of the following:

I .... [your name] hereby accept
Angelic Insurance from my angel ....
[name, if you know it] for the following areas of my life:

– accepting and giving unconditional love
– financial support
– emotional support

and .... [add any other area where you
wish to feel assured of love and affection.]

Then sign your name and date it. You have now created an
Angel Insurance Policy spell. Remember to enjoy all its
benefits!

Every year in the Cognac region of France, barrel upon barrel of brandy lies ageing in oak casks in various distilleries in the district. In one distillery alone, over 700,000 litres of alcohol evaporates into the atmosphere while the brandy matures. Aficionados of brandy might think 'What a waste!' but the distillery owners call this 'the angels' share'.

We often begin a new project with gusto but then its energy evaporates as we lose confidence and interest. We can spend hours, days and weeks with people who never seem to appreciate our presence. When we look at our life in hindsight we can often concentrate only on what we have lost, not what we have gained. But nothing is wasted. We have shared our energy, our thoughts, our love, and that is important. Even if a relationship did not last long, there was something gained on both sides. Rather than feel bereft and abandoned, look back on those experiences and realize what you thought you lost was actually 'the angels' share'.

It's lovely to think of the devas as they work in the garden. You can help them by improving the soil and heightening the plants' ability to thrive by using some simple methods yourself. If you want to have an abundant crop of tomatoes and/or roses, sow some parsley close by. This attracts bees and will therefore help the other plants to be fertilized. Rosemary is good for keeping away carrot fly, and garlic and lavender keep aphids at bay. Chives and nasturtium should be planted around apple trees, and nasturtium keep aphids away from broccoli and tomatoes.

We are neither the light, nor the message.
We are the messengers.
We are nothing. You are, for us, everything.
WIM WENDERS'S *FARAWAY, SO CLOSE!*

Always understand that the angels can only give us guidance to get on the right road and do the right thing. They cannot make us do anything. They can only advise and try to synchronize the backdrop from which we can take action. It is always up to us, not our angels, to take the action!

11 April

When we're aware of the many, many hungry people in the world, we can believe that it's wrong for us to be abundant. So often we feel we should have 'just enough to get by', because it wouldn't be fair to ask for more. However, angels do not believe in limitation and nor should we. By limiting our ability to bring wealth of all kinds into our lives we do not help anyone. If we get poor it does not mean someone else gets rich! The opposite applies, too. Instead, why not ask your angels to help you to accept *More than enough to share and to spare*? By doing so you can then share the surplus with those who are less fortunate than yourself.

There is good reason to love yourself.

ANGEL INSPIRATION

Yes, there is good reason to love yourself, even though you may not believe it right now. Most of us have been brought up thinking that loving oneself is selfish. It's not. You are the only human being who knows you through and through. Your angel also knows you thoroughly. It is vital to learn to love yourself, regardless of the things you did in the past that were wrong, or the things you didn't do, and all those other memories we hold onto in our hearts. Angels know we're doing the best we can. No-one can do better than their best. Ask your angel to help you stop judging yourself. Open up to compassion and love for yourself, then you can share it with others.

13 April

Today is the first day of the Solar (Sun) New Year. Celebrate by making a suncatcher for your home.

All you need is some 'invisible' thread, a narrow needle for threading, clear crystal beads and some coloured beads: red for physical energy, orange for emotional energy, yellow for enthusiasm, green for your heart, blue for communication, indigo/purple for spirit, and pink and white for general health and protection. Begin with the lowest item on the sun-catcher, that is the pendulum or ball-shaped bead, then simply thread the coloured beads intermingled with the clear crystal beads to the design of your choice. Make a strong knot in the thread when you have come to the end, then leave enough thread to make a 'hanger'. Hang it in a place which catches the light best and where it can be spun around, bringing light into your room, just as angels do!

14 April

You haven't lived till you've tried this hot drink, **Fallen Angel**. (Just make sure you're not driving!) Here's how you make it:

Make a cup of strong, preferably real, coffee. Add a measure of Bailey's Irish Cream Liqueur. Stir. Top with whipped cream. Then sprinkle grated chocolate over the top. Now relax and take a sip. Yum! No wonder it's called 'Fallen Angel'!

Our deepest fear is not that we are inadequate ...
it is that we are powerful beyond measure.

MARIANNE WILLIAMSON, *A RETURN TO LOVE*

The Angel of Power is with you today. Does that make you feel nervous? Are you fearful that if we are powerful you may abuse it? Each and every one of us has the ability to accept that power. Power does not have to be abused, not when it's in the right hands. Becoming empowered by opening up to your angel can help you move away from fear and towards your ability to be committed, knowing and loving.

Take up pen and paper today (or word processor) and write that letter you've been promising to write for so long. Whether it's one of rage, of appreciation, of leaving or of love, when you seal the envelope write the letters S.W.A.K. on the back. Those initials stand for 'Sealed With Angel Kisses'. You never know what changes you can bring about because of your deed today.

We never cease to learn, and that is the way it should be as we share knowledge and wisdom with each other at this 'University of Life'. Today, welcome in new knowledge. Ask your angel *'Is there anything I need to know right now?'* Sit quietly and see if you can feel a message coming to you. Don't despair if you don't receive anything just now. Once you've asked this question you will get an answer sometime during the day, and it could come to you in several different ways: via a message on the phone, an overheard conversation, a topic on the radio or a programme on TV.

Think of a song whose lyrics include the word 'angel'. Write out as much of the lyrics as you can remember and ponder on the words. This will bring more awareness of angels into your life on a daily basis. It's even better if you do this with a friend or child. Think about all the people in the world who have been touched by this song. How did it change their lives? Think about how much it changed your life. Then sing it aloud!

It's so important to have a balance in nature, but often we forget, destroying the wild flowers and plants which have just as much right to grow and are often of medicinal worth, too.

Rather than pulling up every weed today, honour them! Everything has a purpose, and most of our conventional medicines are synthetic versions of our weeds and wild flowers. By destroying everything that doesn't fit into our social 'plan', we are often creating problems for ourselves in the future. Apart from that, even those 'weeds' have an angel looking after them, and they should be respected for what they can offer. Take the wild foxglove. It's the origin of digitalis, a drug used to help those with heart problems. Not only does it help humans, it also enhances and stimulates the growth of other plants where it grows. Other 'weeds' which are disappearing are common milkwort, which was used to help nursing mothers, and musk mallow for throat infections and coughs, and camomile was called 'the plants' physician' by the Egyptians because its presence improves the health of everything else in the garden!

The Sun goes into the Earth sign of Taurus today, and it is Archangel Michael who looks after this zodiac sign. Welcome Archangel Michael into your life today and realize that he can help you overcome your deepest fears. He will stand by your side when you need extra help, but it is up to you to face those fears, he cannot force you to do so.

Light a white candle today to honour Archangel Michael. Make sure you have something orange or gold in your life during this month, and every time your eye catches these colours remember that his power is with you.

21 April

When you touch a fellow human being in love,
you are doing God's work.
See within each human being a fallen angel.

PAT RODEGAST AND JUDITH STANTON, *EMMANUEL'S BOOK*

Make it your job today to connect with someone with the healing energy of love. It may be a stranger, it may be someone with whom you normally do not get along. Smile, say 'hello', offer to give a helping hand. Make a difference to that person's life by sharing a memory of God's love together.

April is known for its uncertain weather. It can be both wet and sunny at the same time, and we call this 'April Showers'. Just as the soil needs both rain and sunshine for healthy growth, so do we. We're all here at this 'University of Life' in order to grow spiritually. When we realize that it is just about learning lessons that we come across on our path, rather than major disasters that seem to hold us, stuck in the mud, then we can learn the lesson and move on. Just like at university, once you've learned the lesson and passed the test, you won't have to repeat it!

Spend some time in silence today and ask your angel to help you have an overview of your life at present. Who is presently helping you to face those lessons you need to learn? How can you best react to them? Understanding that these people are here for you to help you learn, look on them now in this different light. Bless them for being in your life.

If you need a loan from a financial institution, remember to invite the Angel of Divine Abundance to walk with you through the doors of that institution as you ask for a loan, or ask that it sits close by as you make that phone call! Before you ask for anything, first say in your head *'The Angel of Divine Abundance goes before me and prepares my way.'* You'll be amazed how many doors open for you from this moment!

Have some fun today and bring about harmony as well! Get some 'angel confetti' and go for a walk around your neighbourhood and carefully leave behind you a tiny confetti angel in places which you feel are in need of angel love.

*Dear George, Remember no man is a failure who
has friends. Thanks for the wings!
Love, Clarence.*

FRANK CAPRA'S *IT'S A WONDERFUL LIFE*

It doesn't matter how much money you have. While having
money is much better than living in poverty, it definitely
does not guarantee happiness! Happiness is a warm feeling of
contentment deep inside. There is no point in pursuing happiness outside of ourselves, for it won't be there, it has to grow
from within.

Today, spend some time thinking back over your life. Think
of the friends you have had, how they have helped you
through difficult times. Take a blue candle and light it, all the
while naming as many of your friends, past and present, who
have given you support in good and bad times.

Time to clear up the garden! Flowers and plants should be blooming and blossoming so it's time to tend and nurture those courageous growths which have battled against the harsh winter nights and days just gone. Why is it that it seems the flowers wilt yet the weeds get stronger and stronger? As I mentioned earlier, it is believed that if you firstly talk to weeds and warn them that you are coming and are going to clear them away they will be much easier to lift from the soil. Use that hoe and gently push away any weeds that have sprouted, making sure you take their roots. If possible, allow a small area of your garden to remain wild.

Spend as much time outdoors as possible today. Go around all the new growth and talk to it and its deva which is looking after it. Give them plenty of encouragement to grow in abundance in the coming weeks.

God doesn't ask us to be perfect.
God asks us only to be present.

ANGEL INSPIRATION

No-one is meant to be perfect. If we were we would not have had to come here to the Planet Earth in the first place! We're all here to learn at the 'University of Life' and so move forward. Not one of us is more advanced than the others.

Give yourself a break today and pat yourself on the head, just for being here! For God doesn't ask us to be perfect, God asks us only to be present. Have a go at things, be willing to do things differently and do different things. You don't have to excel, or even succeed! Just be present and be willing to open up to guidance.

In Roman times this would be the first day of the Festival of Flora, the time when people celebrated the growth and beauty of the flowers of nature around them. Recognizing that we are all part of the same Creation – whether we're human, animal, vegetation or etheric being – will help us all to bring balance back to the Planet. How can we expect growth and harvest where the land has been raped? The more gentle and co-operative we are with the gifts of nature around us, the better the harvest will be.

Start today by thanking the devas who have been working so hard to keep the balance between Nature's needs and the gifts of floral abundance that we can all share. Look at the beauty of each flower and marvel at the miracle which gave this life.

Look back over the last four weeks. Remember you created the feelings of joy, happiness and adventure with the help of your angel and Asmodel, the Angel of April. What has changed for you? What opportunities have you grasped that came your way? Have you acted more spontaneously than before? Thank your angel and Asmodel for bringing you all the opportunities for faith, trust and spiritual growth during this last month. Light a candle to honour their help over the last four weeks.

30 April

As the Sun begins to set today, welcome the Celtic Angel of the West into your life. This angel brings with it the celebration of the Sun's Light, Beltane. Wear bright colours today, especially of orange or yellow to signify the Sun's rays. Beltane is a time for celebration, acknowledging the cycles of nature and our own fertility. We can see that the effort we put into our springtime is now beginning to reward us and Mother Nature is working away on our behalf. Time to have a break, meet with friends, relax after a demanding few months. Exchange news, tell each other of your own angel experiences at this time. Enjoy the festival of friendship and peace with the Angel of the West.

In the Southern Hemisphere, today is the Celtic festival of Samhain, the start of the New Year (see 31 October).

The Angel of May

Ambiel

(Southern Hemisphere - Ambiel is the Angel of November)

1 May

All around us at this time there is abundance. The Angel of May, Ambiel, is busy encouraging growth throughout this month. Remember to greet the devas every day and thank them for taking over the work for us. Light a green candle and welcome Ambiel into your life. This is a wonderful time to enjoy creative pursuits, preferably out of doors. During May you may enjoy the growth of abundance in your own bank account as well! Ask Angel Ambiel to help you cultivate a healthy attitude to yourself, to your sense of self-worth, which will then manifest in financial worth.

The restrictions of the winter months are over and we can begin to see the effort we put into our spring beginning to grow and blossom. For the full month of May all over the Northern Hemisphere we celebrate the growth of flowers in our gardens and in our fields.

Make a special effort to gather flowers, wild or cultivated, and put them in a vase, in a special place, to honour your angels. Be sure to talk to the flowers and welcome them into your home, and tell them they have been chosen as a gift for your angels. Keep this vase filled with flowers all through the month of May as a gesture of thanks and celebration.

3 May

The emerald is the crystal associated with the month of May. These stones, which are part of the beryl variety, are highly valued. If you can't afford to have an emerald in your life, then jade, malachite or dioptase crystals can be substituted.

These crystals all have healing properties, and are also capable of enhancing our sense of abundance and harmony. Place your chosen stone in your indoor Angel Shrine or bring it with you to the workplace for healthy relationships and co-operation.

Angels fly high 'cos they take themselves lightly.

ANGEL INSPIRATION

Look into a mirror today and look deeply into your eyes. Now smile. Smile and watch your eyes crinkle up and your mouth turn into a big grin. Now, doesn't that feel better? Learn to laugh at yourself every now and again, and then, like the angels, you will be able to 'fly higher' and get things into perspective.

5 May

Around this time of abundance you may be tempted to go 'over the top' in areas where you have some addiction. I came across a version of the following ritual on the internet and find it is a very powerful exercise to use in order to free ourselves from negative behaviour patterns:

Sit quietly and consider any addictive or negative behaviour pattern you'd like to release. This exercise is powerful and is going to work, so get ready to make other changes in your life when you've freed yourself from this. (Don't be surprised, however, if you go on a binge of negative behaviour once more after this. There's no need to worry, it's just the 'last gasp'!)

Imagine that the addictive items are sitting on your lap or on a table in front of you. Then, see or feel them floating about one foot in front of your tummy. You see cords extending from your tummy to the addictive items.

Say to yourself that you are now willing to release these things, once and for all. Commit yourself to releasing them.

Now ask Archangel Raphael, who heals the physical body, to cut those cords completely. Imagine him using golden scissors to cut them. As the cords are gently cut, notice the items fall away easily from you. Archangel Raphael takes them away, and as he touches them they turn into light and disappear. You are now free of them. Now Raphael will surround you with an emerald green light to heal you completely.

What colours were the cords? These are some of the things particular colours symbolize:

Red: energy, sexuality, anger. Are you suppressing these in your life?

Orange: emotional support. Do you feel supported or victimized?

Yellow: enthusiasm and attitude. Do you encourage negative or positive thoughts in your life?

Green: love. Do you lack love? How can you open up to love?

Blue: integrity and communication. Do you feel people will listen to you and truly accept you as you are?

Purple: spiritual fulfilment. Do you feel you're doing something of worth, or do you feel 'What's the point?'

Pink/white: self-esteem and acceptance. How do you truly feel about yourself? Do you have a healthy self-esteem?

How are your finances? We may feel angels are too 'heavenly' to be involved here, but they know that money is an important part of our lives, too. Yes, angels can help you sort out your finances so that they are flourishing healthily.

Our financial worth is very much based on our own sense of self-worth. No matter how hard you work at something that makes you feel worthless, you will never be a person of worth. Ask your angel to help you find the right things to do in your life to help you feel like a person of worth (whether you are paid for them or not). In that way your sense of self-worth will increase and so, too, will your financial worth.

If you have any particular debts at present causing concern, put a picture or a figurine of an angel sitting on this bill. Try to divorce your mind from the worry and leave it to the angels to sort it out in the perfect way for you. Soon you should find what once seemed an unsolvable worry is now something that is manageable.

... angels come with a rush and a rustle into the room,
or show their magnificence dancing on a laundry line.

HARRIET SCOTT CHESSMAN

When I first asked my angel its name I sat quietly with my eyes closed and heard a name. I thought it was 'Laura', and my immediate reaction was 'I must have imagined it, that's my niece's name.' Then I saw, in my mind's eye, a line of white squares hanging up like washing on a line, and the letters L-O-R-I-E-L (Loriel) were spelt out for me. (Later I learned that the suffix –el or –il is the old Hebrew word for 'God', so you will notice that all angel names mentioned in the Bible end with this suffix.)

You can get the name of your angel in one of several ways: like me, you might actually hear a name being given. You may see it written down. Or you may just feel a name pop right into your head. Whatever happens, accept the first name that comes into your head, that is the name your angel wishes to be called.

Hawthorn (also known as mayflower) and lily of the valley are the flowers for May. If you travel around ancient sacred sites in the UK and Ireland you will find many fields with a single gnarled hawthorn tree standing on a hillock. These trees tell us that there is a sacred well or sacred energy or 'ley line' where it stands. Do greet the devas who look after these often ignored yet very special trees which give us the heady scent of summer in their flowers at their head, and the deep intimacy of spiritual flow in their roots.

Leave gentle fingerprints on the soul of another
for the angels to read.

ANGEL INSPIRATION

Sometimes we look for angels in our lives and wonder why they don't seem close by. We must remember that the way to connect more easily with them is to 'do as angels do'. It's important to remember that for every action we make, there is a reaction. Whoever you are in contact with today, touch them as though you are an angel. Be gentle, reassuring and understanding. In that way we shall 'leave gentle fingerprints' for the angels to read.

10 May

Make a mandala today. The ancients knew that any intent which was put into a magic circle (a mandala) would be fulfilled, so when you make this mandala for yourself, remember the old saying 'Be careful what you wish for because it will come true'!

You will need a sheet of plain paper (A4 size) and felt-tip pens or crayons. Fold the paper diagonally at the top left-hand corner and the bottom right-hand corner and make a crease. Now open it up and this time fold it from the right-hand corner at the top to the left-hand corner at the bottom, and make a crease. Open it. You now have the page divided into four quadrants. Draw a large oval right to the edges of the page, then draw another smaller oval inside this (approximately 5 cm/2 inches in diameter). Where the creases appear, draw lines to delineate the quadrants. Now draw a symbol in the centre of the small oval depicting your long-term focus. You could, for example, show yourself being surrounded by angels, or unfolding with knowledge and beauty such as a lotus flower ... use your imagination.

The top quadrant is for your spiritual needs, the quadrant at the bottom is for your physical needs, the right quadrant is for emotional needs, and the left is for intellectual development. Think of what you would love to have in these four areas and draw some symbols in each quadrant of the things you want. For instance, in the right quadrant (emotional needs) you could draw two hearts entwined to symbolize love, or the glyphs for Venus and Mars for sexual compatibility. In the bottom quadrant (physical needs), what about the signs for money (Euro/£/$) or a sketch of a house or car? In the left quadrant (intellectual needs), you could draw a furled diploma, or a variety of books; and in the topmost quadrant, which is about spirituality, what about cats for psychic ability and angels ... the list is endless. What you want is up to you, so trust yourself, and enjoy the exercise! Use as many colours as possible, and have as much fun as possible. Then sign it and date it. You can either put your mandala away in a private place or hang it on the wall. You'll be amazed how these things will come into reality for you!

Go outside into the country today if you can. Take a good look around you at the fields full of growth and the promise of plenty. Feel what it's like to be part of that growth. Try to imagine what it's like to have the breeze ripple through you, the sunlight shine on you ... be part of that natural abundance. Thank the angels for working together with the soil and us humans to bring about these fields full of ripening crops.

12 May

I was listening to the voices of life chanting in unison.

JOHN TRUDELL

Be adventurous! Set your alarm for 4 am and get outside into your garden or into a country place as quickly as you can and listen to the dawn chorus. It starts at approximately 4.25 am today, and will begin with just one bird's call. Then another answers and another ... before long the whole planet is alive with birdsong! It is believed in some cultures that the dawn chorus wakens the Earth and all the beings on it to begin to grow and flourish, and the night chorus sends them to sleep.

Allow yourself to waken to your inner chorus of joy as you listen to the growing chorus of thousands of birds bringing the planet back to life again!

(Readers in the Southern Hemisphere should put 12 November in their diary for the dawn chorus.)

Isn't it interesting how we often overlook the obvious when we're going through difficult times? One simple little ritual which you can carry out once a month, or whenever you feel the need, is to use the gifts from nature to help your bank balance along. Just put a dab of bergamot or peppermint essential oil on your bank book, cheque book, post office savings book, and so on, and you'll soon notice how the money seems to multiply rather than disappear. After all, money comes from a 'mint', doesn't it!

As I mentioned earlier, there are little bags of 'angel confetti' available in the shops nowadays, and if you place one or two of these little angel symbols in your bank books and your purse, you'll find that financial worry flies out of the window if you let it.

Crystals can also act like magnets to draw money to you. Carry a small citrine stone in your purse and you'll soon find it is never empty. (A citrine 'tumble stone' should cost very little.) If you can't find citrine, choose any gold-coloured stone.

Angels, in the early morning
May be seen the Dews among
Stooping – plucking – smiling – flying
Do the Buds to them belong?

EMILY DICKINSON

Make an effort today to get up early and spend time in the quiet of the dawn. Look on the beauty of nature around you with new eyes; imagine you can see the angels dancing in the morning light.

Have you still some angel confetti to share? Surprise some-one today by inserting a tiny piece of angel confetti into something they will find, perhaps a handbag, a cheque book, a car's glove compartment, a lunch box ... use your imagina-tion and realize how you can help to bring a sparkle of love into someone's life today!

Make some **Angel Fishcakes** today. It's really easy and can help to encourage young children in particular to enjoy this wholesome food.

For 15 Angel Fishcakes you will need:

450 g/1 lb cooked fish (your own preference)

450 g/1 lb mashed potato

2 large eggs, beaten

2 tablespoons lemon juice

salt and pepper

55 g/2 oz breadcrumbs

Mix the mashed potato with the cooked fish. Add half of the beaten egg to bind it, with the lemon juice, and season to taste with salt and pepper. Take a spoonful of the mixture, roll with your hand and shape into an angel with wings. Brush with the remainder of the beaten egg and cover in breadcrumbs. Fry, bake or grill as for ordinary fish cakes until they are golden.

17 May

A fine thing to be talking about angels in this day when common thieves smash the holy rosaries of their victims in the street ...

JACK KEROUAC, *DESOLATION ANGELS*

Do not lose heart. The one thing we all have is free will, and that means the angels cannot stop people behaving in a particular way. However, when we consciously invite angelic love and guidance into our lives we are immediately in tune with the knowledge of where to go, where to stay away from, who to spend time with, and who to avoid. All we need to do is listen to the advice and take it!

18 May

Have a picnic today no matter what the weather and invite your angel to join you! You can just as easily enjoy the adventure of a picnic at home, indoors if it rains, as go on a long journey in the countryside! A picnic is all about freedom of choice and letting go of the usual conformity of dining. Look on today as an adventure – do something different, eat something different, have a go at something new! It's amazing how your attitude to life can change when you look on your circumstances from a different vantage point. Remember to lay a place for your angel and have a happy time conversing together!

Find a 'power object' today. A 'power object' is something which seems to speak to you, which makes you feel better and stronger and more empowered because you have it. It may be anything: a book, a ribbon, a feather, a bit of flotsom from the beach. You may find it immediately, you may have to search for it. Don't worry if it's the latter, that's just the angels helping you be more aware of your need to have things which are meaningful; to prove that, like most things in life, the more effort you put in, the more you get out! When you have found your power object, you should honour it by keeping it in a special place and treating it with gratitude and respect.

Every raindrop that falls is accompanied by an Angel,
for even a raindrop is a manifestation of being.

MOHAMMED

Every raindrop, every snowflake, every blade of grass has an angel. As the Australian Aborigines say, we are part of the Earth and the Earth is part of us, therefore we must appreciate and respect everything around us.

Today is the first day of the zodiac sign of Gemini, the twins. Archangel Uriel presides over this zodiac sign, encouraging us to communicate with one another with integrity and loving kindness. The more we connect with Archangel Uriel and invite him to look after us, our homes, workplaces and community areas, the better our lives will be. We must be proactive ourselves in ensuring the expansion of cosmic consciousness, that is understanding that we're all here as humans and each of us has a spirit which is on a journey of enlightenment.

Wear the colours white or indigo today, and burn a blue candle to invite Archangel Uriel to be part of your life for the next month.

In his book, *Parting Visions*, Dr Melvin Morse says that in his own research at least 50% of children in his studies see 'guardian angels' as a part of their near-death experiences. And that's not all; he found that later these angels may reappear to the same people in order to help in times of crisis.

When you are speaking to children today, why not bring up the subject of angels and see how they react? You may be amazed at the experiences they share with you! (Don't forget to share your own experiences with them, too.)

23 May

Open a book at random today. By doing so you can open up to all sorts of interesting messages and unexpected pieces of information. Go to a bookshop, visit a library, or simply pick a book from your own shelves. Hold the book close to your heart. Ask your angel to guide you to find the message you need at this moment. Now open the book and point your finger on a page at random. Open your eyes and read the message. What does it mean to you? Place it in your heart and go back to it now and again today.

24 May

How will today go for you? Will it be an uphill battle or an enjoyable experience? Although it's sometimes difficult to accept, it is important to remember that each of us has the freedom of choice. While none of us can stop it raining or snowing, each can make a choice as to how we respond to that weather. Do we stay dry or do we get wet? It's our choice. Similarly, we are in charge of the outcome of each new day. We can say 'yes' or we can say 'no'. Archangel Uriel can help you make positive choices in every area of your life. Choose to respond to one specific aspect differently from today.

Find your strength in love.

ANGEL INSPIRATION

It is only by going through difficulties that we become strong.
By opening up to love when we are facing such trials we can
understand that we are not alone but have the unconditional
support that we need from our angels.

26 May

Go on a sightseeing tour of your hometown today. Start with churches, and move on to shops and private houses. See how many sculptures, names and window displays contain something to do with an angel. You'll be surprised!

When you commit your ideas and beliefs to the written word you are giving them even more power. With the angels' help we can use 'The 5-Steps Ritual' to help us accept financial abundance. You will need a sheet of tinted paper (either green, purple or one that has some gold on it), a pen that writes with gold ink or a narrow paintbrush and gold ink, and an envelope. (If you cannot get gold ink, use a green or purple felt-tip pen.) All you have to do now is decide how much money you wish to have.

Now follow these five steps:

'Dear Archangel Gabriel (or Parasiel),

I, ... [your name], make a conscious decision to accept Euro/£/$ .... or more into my life right now.

I commit myself to accepting Euro/£/$ .... or more into my life right now.

I affirm that I now have Euro/£/$ .... or more in my life right now.

Thank you, Archangel Gabriel (or Parasiel), for helping me attain Euro/£/$ .... or more in my life right now.

I now let go and leave this request in the hands of the angels.'

Now sign your full name and put the date on the letter. Place the letter in the envelope, put an angel picture or figurine sitting on it or close by it, and let the angels do the rest for you. The main thing is to leave it up to them at this point. Don't interfere; just accept with gratitude.

28 May

When they count my sins in heaven, then
I'll get to know my luck.
Is it furnace no. 7, or a harp for me to pluck?
BERTOLT BRECHT, *HAPPY END*

Studies on people who have undergone 'near-death experiences' show that we are given the opportunity to review our life and see the effects of our actions. There is no judgement from the spirit, it is only ourselves who are the judge and jury. From today, don't waste time in judgement; just try not to repeat any negative actions.

An eminent theologian in the University of Birmingham, Emma Heathcote, has studied several hundred people's experiences of 'meeting' with angels. She discovered that 25% saw their angel with wings, and 20% met their angel in human form, who appeared suddenly and, just as suddenly, disappeared. The remainder felt a presence, smelled an unusual perfume, saw a figure in white, or felt enveloped in an angel's wings. Though children being very psychic and open find such meetings an everyday occurrence, Ms Heathcote's studies referred to adults aged between 36 and 55 years.

As I always tell the participants in my workshops, don't expect an angel in white with an impressive wingspan and a golden halo to appear in front of you! Yes, it could happen, but it's much more likely to show itself in a more gentle, less awe-inspiring way. After all, it knows your fears and doesn't want to frighten you! How have you connected with your angel? Have you seen a bright light, felt the strength of its wings, found a feather, enjoyed the essence of a flower or perfume in an unusual place?

How is your Earth Shrine progressing? Make sure you water the flowers when necessary and give them some extra fertilizer, if you wish. There are still quite a few seeds and plants you can add to it, if you have the space. Now is the time to consider planting for winter colour. There are several winter-flowering heathers in purple, pink or white that will not only bring you colour but also offer pollen to any hardworking bees in your neighbourhood. There's also michelmas daisies, winter jasmine, and even late-flowering nasturtiums which will last up to the first frosts. Quieten your mind and ask the devas to help you perfect your Earth Shrine.

31 May

Thank Ambiel, the Angel of May, for all her gifts of abundance. While you may still be waiting for your pockets and purse to be full, bear in mind that everything needs time to grow and produce fruit. Be patient. Keep thanking Ambiel and your other angels for their help and support. Also, money is just a symbol of wealth, and perhaps you have other wealth in your life which cannot be bought with money and which you may have overlooked. Have you loving family, friends, supportive colleagues, neighbours ...?

The Angel of June

Muriel

(Southern Hemisphere - Muriel is the Angel of December)

1 June

June is a wonderful month. It's a perfect time for rest and relaxation after all the effort of spring and early summer. You can see it was well worth the effort now! The Angel for June is Muriel and this angel can help us make the most of this abundant month. We can see our gardens grow and blossom but it's not yet time to pick our fruit. Nature is really at her best as we are offered the peace and stability of knowing that our harvest is guaranteed later on. We may need to pluck some weeds from our abundant growth, and spend some time fertilizing and pruning, and Muriel can help us enjoy these tasks in the company of loving and supportive friends and family under the light of the Summer Solstice towards the end of the month.

Light an orange candle today to celebrate the gift of growth that Angel Muriel brings us. Remember the devas are at their busiest at this time in the gardens and fields, so spare a thought for them while you put your feet up and relax a little!

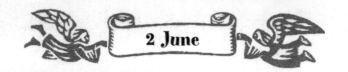

Pearl is the crystal for the month of June. Think of how it is formed: a tiny grain of sand enters an oyster shell and, because of this invasion, the oyster responds to what it sees as an attack and so the beautiful pearl is formed.

Consider the adage 'pearls of wisdom'. We receive these in our own hearts through facing the 'invasions' of others in our life. We are often forced to respond to someone's seeming 'attack' yet from that response we develop wisdom.

Look back into your past. How far have you moved forward in self-awareness and spiritual development because you were forced into change through an apparent 'attack' or 'invasion' by an outside source? Ask your angel to help you to look at your present situation with new, aware eyes. Is there any 'attack' or 'invasion' going on in your life now which can, in reality, give you the gift of 'pearls of wisdom'?

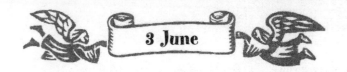

If you're travelling anywhere today why not put an imaginary ribbon of protection around your car, or the train, bus or plane in which you are? Just imagine your vehicle has a big pink or white ribbon tied in a bow around it, as though it's been gift-wrapped. You can also imagine that Archangel Michael is in front of you, protecting the path as you move forward. Always remember to surround yourself with an aura of protective energy; it's just a thought away and can keep you and your loved ones safe and secure.

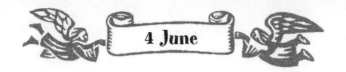

Forget anger toward all who have offended you,
For from anger springs a multitude of wrongs.
The face's smile and the heart's joy are slain by anger.
Does there exist a greater enemy than one's own anger?

TIRUKKURAL 31: 303–304

It is human to feel anger, but holding on to it does nothing but quench the light in your life. When you feel anger building up inside you, do not become a victim of it, instead ask your angel to help you express it in the most positive way. Sometimes writing a letter to the media can be the answer, at other times the anger can get you to act in a way that is self-empowering. If your anger is directed at someone close to you, you can also write them a letter expressing all the vitriolic you feel, but do not under any circumstances send it to them! Instead, light a candle, ask your angel to help you let go of that anger, then burn the letter. In this way you're 'sending it to the light' in order for it to be healed. Don't feel guilty about your letter to your loved one, instead feel relieved and free!

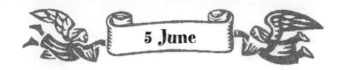

5 June

When you see the honeysuckle or a rose blooming remember that these are the flowers of June. Greet them, touch them gently and enjoy their fragrance. The devas looking after the roses really like to have the energy of the rose quartz crystal close by. You can also enhance the flowers by watering them with gem water, which is water charged with the added properties of, in this instance, rose quartz.

To make up some gem water (which lasts 2–3 days):

Sterilize a glass jar/jug with boiling water and then fill it with distilled or spring water and add the crystal of your choice. Leave the jar/jug outside (with a lid on) on the soil for 24 hours if possible, where it can benefit from the rays of the Sun and the Moon. Before you use this special water, bless it and thank the devas for helping to charge this water with the power of the crystal.

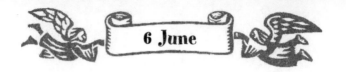

To err is human, to forgive divine.

ALEXANDER POPE

No-one's perfect, we're not meant to be. Remind yourself today not to judge yourself or others. Just learn from your mistakes!

Have you ever felt the negative influence of other people in your life? It's important to realize that everyone has an aura, or energy field, and we can each affect others by that energy that we carry with us. We can protect ourselves from other people's negative energy field by imagining an eggshell around us. That eggshell can be plain white, or any colour or design you wish it to be. Stand up and feel conscious of your feet touching the Earth below. Now imagine that the eggshell is surrounding your energy field. It's completely covering you from head to foot. Now you can go anywhere today without being affected by anyone you meet. Your angel can feel closer to you now because there isn't anyone else's energy coming between you.

If you have children in your life, explain how they can imagine a shield is protecting them from any negative influences approaching them, and that their angel is standing behind them at all times. In this way you can ensure that they don't become victims of bullying or violence.

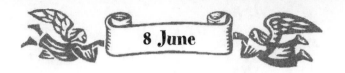

8 June

Angels may not always come when you call them,
but they will always come when you need them.

ANON

Try not to make the mistake of thinking your angel will do the required work for you! This is quite a common belief, and one which can result in a feeling of great disappointment. Remember that angels are the messengers who suggest change, not the instigators of change. It is up to us to put things into action, and we'll never be alone, though we must take that first step ourselves ...!

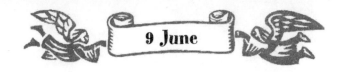

9 June

Do you remember the TV programme *Stairway to Heaven?* What about the more recent *Touched By an Angel?* These were innocent yet inspired TV serials which brought the idea of angels into the lives of millions of people. Like the fables of old, each had a 'moral' or a 'karmic outcome'. See if you can find a re-run of one of these shows and watch it with fresh eyes. If not, mention the series to friends and bring back some beloved memories of angels helping out when times get tough.

10 June

Be strong and courageous.

DANIEL 10:18, THE BIBLE

It's so important to understand that when things go apparently 'wrong' in our lives it is all about learning lessons. The
quicker we learn, the quicker the need to learn that lesson
disappears. But why is it that angels cannot sort it out for us?
It is because they have no power to force us to do anything,
to take away our free will.

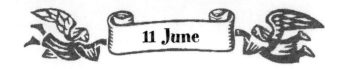

Be the change you want to see in the world.

MAHATMA GANDHI

Yes, you are the one who is responsible for your own little patch of this Earth. None of us can expect the outside world to change without our help. By offering ourselves as the instigator of change, the world around us can change. We can shout and yell and demand change outside of ourselves, but it is only when we are willing to change that our world will change in reality.

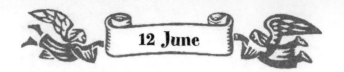

12 June

Go to an art gallery today and see how many pictures show angels. Bring children along with you if you can, they tend to be much more observant than adults! Make it into a game and keep scores.

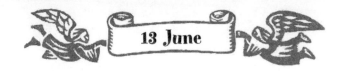

Enjoy this exercise to bring more abundance into your life. Record it first if you like:

Begin by taking some deep breaths and, as you breathe out, let go of any chattering in your mind. Now imagine there's a gentle waterfall above you showering you with a beautiful golden light, starting at your head and moving all the way down to your feet. You find yourself standing at the gateway outside a walled garden. You open the gate and step inside. Know that your angel is with you here today.

You realize you're in an orchard. You see lots of people about, each with their angel. You follow your angel down a path. You pass many people busy collecting their harvest from their trees. Your angel says that everyone has their own tree, including you.

You are excited. In the near distance one tree seems to stand out. Its branches are laden with all sorts of strange fruits. As you come closer, you see the branches aren't carrying fruits, they're carrying money! Your angel explains that this is your special tree. Everything on it is yours!

You find a receptacle to carry away your harvest. Your angel tells you to shake the tree. You do so. It feels heavy. Now money starts falling down around you. It seems a waterfall is showering you with abundance! There's notes, and coins, and cheques. You begin to collect your harvest in your receptacle. Soon it is filled with abundance, yet there is plenty more still on the tree.

Your angel says you can come back and shake any branch when you need more abundance. You feel wonderful as you leave this tree behind, returning to the path and finding yourself once more breathing in deeply, all the way down to your feet, and now you open up your eyes and return to your room feeling much more abundant than ever before!

14 June

Friends are quiet angels who lift us to our feet
when our wings have trouble remembering how to fly.

ANON

A true friend is someone who won't always agree with you! A true friend will not let you wallow in feelings of victim-consciousness. A true friend is someone who will remind you that you have a purpose in life and will support you as you try to achieve that sense of purpose. Bless every friend you have, whether you have just one or many. Where would you be without them?

15 June

Make up a Gratitude List today. Mention everyone who, so far this year, has come into your life and taught you something. (That doesn't mean just the 'nice' people, often we learn most from those who seem to make our life a misery! Remember it's all about being here at this 'University of Life' and learning on our way.) Keep the list going from today onwards, and add to it every week. You'll be amazed at how much you've gained and learned from everyone who passes through your life. (Remember to add your angels to the list too!)

Did you ever say the following prayer? If you have a young child you may like to teach it to them so that they need never fear the darkness of the night.

Matthew, Mark, Luke and John,
Bless the bed that I lay on.
Four corners to my bed,
Four angels 'round me spread:
One at the head, one at the feet
And two to guard me while I sleep ...

17 June

Be a good neighbour and visit someone unexpectedly. Offer to do their shopping, their ironing, even weed their garden for them or cook them a meal! Whatever it is, make sure you're doing it with your heart. Smile!

18 June

Get some sheets of paper (a roll of wallpaper lining is perfect for this) and some finger paints. These items are very reasonably priced so you can really go to town on being creative! Invite friends around, or involve children, and spend at least part of the day painting angels, flowers, devas ... Ask Archangel Gabriel, who looks after the creative arts, to join you in your pursuit.

... there was a flutter of wings and the
bright appearance of an angel in the air,
speeding forth on some heavenly mission.

NATHANIAL HAWTHORNE, *THE CELESTIAL RAILROAD*

Take some time to meditate alone today. Play some gentle music in the background and sit comfortably, making sure you will not be distracted. Let go of any anxious thoughts. Tell your thinking mind that you can deal with these things later on, but just for now you're going on a little break away from your normal daily concerns.

Imagine that you have no body. You are just spirit, floating through the air, with nothing to keep you stuck back on Earth. Imagine you're gently moving with an air thermal, some distance from your home, high in the skies above. Enjoy this feeling of freedom for 15–20 minutes. Then slowly return back to Earth and into your body, moving through your head all the way down the torso and into the soles of your feet.

20 June

The triumph of anything is a matter of organisation.
If there are such things as angels I hope they are
organised along the lines of the Mafia.

KURT VONNEGUT, *SIRENS OF TITAN*

Although we can see much negativity via our TV screens, there is great hope for our planet now that more and more people are opening up to angels. I term people who have come to my workshops and are spreading the word about angels as 'Margaret's Mafia'! I do believe we can just as successfully bring positive energy into the world as others can bring negative energy.

Today think of others in your life who believe the same as yourself about angelic help and the ability to create joyful, happy lives with their help. Start your own 'mafia' of angel believers. Don't 'hide your light under a bushel'; come out of the closet and speak about your beliefs!

An angel, robed in spotless white,
Bent down and kissed the sleeping Night,
Night woke to blush; the sprite was gone,
Men saw the blush and called it Dawn.

PAUL LAURENCE DUNBAR

In the Northern Hemisphere, today is the Summer Solstice when the Sun seems to stay stationary in the skies above us. (If you live in the Southern Hemisphere, you will be celebrating the Winter Solstice today, while the Summer Solstice falls on 21 December.) It is therefore the longest day of the year, when we have the least amount of darkness.

Make the most of today, the day when the Sun has the most power during the 12 calendar months. Get up and about as early as possible and greet the dawn in the east. Wear yellow or orange, the colours of sunshine. Thank the Sun for all its benefits in our lives. Burn a yellow or orange candle as you watch the Sun set into the west.

This is the first day of the Sun sign Cancer, symbolized by the Crab. The Crab, which has a hard shell but soft interior, side-steps issues and finds it difficult to face conflict or change. This Water sign is looked after by Archangel Gabriel, who can help us all discover our psychic and sensitive nature, and so help to bring natural justice to our world with love and nurturing. Being closely associated with the Moon, this is a time when family sensitivites come to the fore.

Whatever your zodiac sign, wear the colours silver, white and blue during the next month of this sign as a reminder that Archangel Gabriel is looking after us all on the Planet Earth. When you are asking for protection for your family from Archangel Gabriel, light a candle and imagine each member surrounded by a beam of silver light coming down from Heaven.

23 June

Today is Midsummer Day in the Northern Hemisphere. This date was set into the formal calendar as an official date to celebrate the middle of the pastoral season. In Celtic times it was the festival of Tara, the central place of Ireland which was dedicated to legalities, justice and peacemaking. While the harvest grew and flourished, the people would come together to make agreements for their peaceful future.

Ask the Angel of Divine Peace to come into your life today. Think of someone who has in some way hurt you. See them clearly in your mind's eye. Ask your angel and the Angel of Divine Peace to be with you as you say the person's name aloud and then *'The Light within me salutes the Light within you.'* See how free you feel afterwards! That is what peace is all about, and it must start within each of us.

You're never alone, you've an angel,
Although it may seem far away:
Somewhere up in the sky, above where the clouds fly,
But that's where they come from, not where they reside,
You just have to call them to be by your side
'Cos you're never alone, you've an angel.

MARGARET NEYLON

No matter how difficult and lonely life may seem on occasion, do remember you really are never alone. You always have that angelic presence by your side, guiding you and supporting you along the right path in life. Remember to ask for your angel's help. It's a verbal commitment you're making to yourself to bring about the changes that you need to make your life fulfilled and happy.

From today, every time you see or hear someone behaving in a way that is at odds with angelic love, say in your mind *'The Light within me salutes the Light within you.'* In that way you are contacting their spiritual, higher selves. You are bypassing their fearful, angry ego and instead encouraging their Light within to shine. It may take some time for that fearful person to reconnect with their Light, but at least you know you have helped them take the first faltering steps in the right direction.

If you feel uncertain of the next step to take, spend some time in silence today. Sit quietly, ask your angel to be with you to bring you the gift of clarity into your life. Let your mind drift while concentrating on the 'gut reaction' that you are receiving. It is a feeling, rather than a thought, and it is coming from your intuition, which is 'tuition from within', knowledge from your spirit.

Even if you haven't felt any specific answer after these moments of meditation, realize that you have unconsciously created a 'blueprint' to follow which will put you on the path that is right for you.

27 June

All the Utopia will come to pass only when
we grow wings and all people are converted into angels.

FEDOR DOSTOEVSKY, *THE DIARY OF A WRITER*

Can you imagine what it would be like to grow wings? Sit quietly where you are now and just imagine little wings beginning to grow outwards from your spine. Imagine that they are growing outwards in either direction. How heavy do they seem to you? Are they offering you a burden or a sense of freedom? What would it be like to truly fly? How warm or how cold does the wind feel as you move upwards and onwards with the help of your wings? Enjoy the sensation!

Angels are 'beings of light' and they don't have bodies or feathered wings. I believe that the reason we have painted angels with wings over the centuries is because we knew they were from 'above', i.e. the higher vibration, and the only way we could imagine them travelling from Heaven down to Earth was to give them wings, just like the birds who fly above us.

Angels understand our beliefs about them, so often show their presence to us by leaving feathers behind. They can be small or large, white, brown or black, fluffy or straight. Numerous people have told me that, in their darkest hour, they found a feather in an unusual place which gave them the strength to go on.

Is there any area in your life where angelic influences could bring about improvements? If so, look out for a feather in an unusual place. Carry it with you in your wallet or purse. Whenever your see it, remember your angels are always close by, helping you to iron out problems in the most loving way.

29 June

I grew up as a female who heard voices.

LUCILLE CLIFTON

On 29 June, 1994, I was lying in my garden in Dublin, looking up at the sky, when a voice said distinctly: *'Give a course called Talking with Angels.'* I recognized the voice because I've heard it so often over the years. It was the voice of my angel.

Though I hadn't a clue how to go about it, I took the plunge and advertised my new course, committing myself to a date six weeks ahead. I still didn't know how to run it so I asked for help from my angels, and they replied in many ways: I was prompted to pick up specific books and magazines at random in which I found many unexpected references to angels, and during my sleeping hours I was given a lot of guidance.

Since that date my life has changed utterly, all for the better. You, too, can listen to the voice of your angel and transform your life beyond your wildest dreams!

Thank Angel Muriel for all the gifts you have received during the month of June. Go outside into your garden or your favourite park and breathe in the luscious scents of mid-summer growth. This is the time of year for enjoying the long summer days with others, when we can all pause and take time out for fun and relaxation, which is so essential for a balanced, contented life. Light an orange candle today to say *'thanks and goodbye for another year'* to Angel Muriel.

Have you been keeping your Angel Journal since January? Now that we are halfway through the calendar year it is a good time to see how much has been going on in your life and how it has changed since the beginning of the year. Perhaps you would like to look through it before you go to sleep tonight.

The Angel of July

Verchiel

(Southern Hemisphere - Verchiel is the Angel of January)

Slow down and take a break for yourself! Verchiel, the Angel of July, is here to remind us that life is about a balance of work and play. Often we are so busy working and pushing ourselves forward that we forget to stop and simply stare. We need to slow down in order to enjoy and appreciate the benefits of the sometimes backbreaking work we have put into our lives. Spend some time outside today if possible, just lazily enjoying the growth around you and listening to the background hum of the bees in the air.

If you made an Earth Shrine earlier in the year, greet the flowers and plants and, of course, their devas. As dusk begins to fall, light some night-lights in your Earth Shrine. (If it's windy, place them in protective containers.) It's really magical to watch the lights dancing in the evening gloaming.

Our deeds fashion our destiny,
Heaven and Hell are in our own hands.

HILLEL

We can rage against Fate, we can believe we've been cursed, but it will never take away the fact that we are responsible for our own lives. If we wish to live in Heaven, we can create it now. If we wish to live in Hell, we can create it now. Every action has a consequence. Staying silent when we should speak out has a consequence. Showing forgiveness has a consequence. Learning to say 'no' has a consequence. Sharing love with someone has a consequence.

No matter what happened in the past it is the past, not the present. Ask your angel to help you to see the past for what it is. Ask for extra help for you to make the changes that are necessary to bring about Heaven on Earth.

The regal crown holds crystals of different colours and value because each crystal symbolizes something special. July's crystal is the highly prized ruby, signifying authority and courage. If you don't own one, use a Carnelian for this exercise:

'Authority' holds within it the word 'author', and each of us should be the author of our own 'book of life'. Sit quietly and go through your present situation. Do you need extra courage, extra decision-making abilities? Your angel is here to help you, but perhaps you need some extra help, something you can physically hold as you face your fear of speaking out and being true to yourself. Hold the crystal in your hands and look deeply into it. Breathe in its red energy into your own heart and mind. All crystals have their own energy and it can be transferred to you when you need it most. Carry the red crystal in your pocket, or wear it in a ring or on a necklace. Each time you see it or touch it, remember you are carrying with you the symbol of your own authority.

4 July

Watch out, there's an angel about!

ANGEL INSPIRATION

When I give workshops or talks I often have members of the audience say they have seen bright flashes of light around me. I believe these flashes of light are the angels trying to get our attention! The reason they congregate around me is because I am the centre of attention at that time as I am giving the workshop. Sometimes we may feel we have to see an angel with white wings and a halo, but I believe the angels are simply 'beings of light' from the 'light source' (in other words, God), and therefore they travel at the speed of light and are made of light. Once you begin to open up to angels don't be in the slightest way surprised if you seem to see flashes of light flying by you, or circles of light bouncing along the walls. These are your angels, 'beings of light', who travel at the speed of light. Watch out, they're around you now. Enjoy their presence!

Go through this book, cheat a little by dipping into the months ahead, and pick out some 'Angel Inspiration' messages that you like. Then make some Angel Inspiration cards, writing the messages out in your own handwriting. All you need is some coloured cardboard, glitter, glue, pen and scissors. Read the words carefully. What do they mean to you? Take your time making your Inspiration Cards and weave love and joy into the words you write. It's even more fun if you make the cards with someone else, adult or child.

Use these Angel Inspiration cards daily. Perhaps keep them in the kitchen so that every morning at breakfast each member of the household can pick a message for the day ahead. All you need to do is shuffle them, ask for a little angelic help today, then choose one with your eyes closed. It's a great habit to get into, and it helps introduce the presence of angels into everyone's life.

The water lily is the flower of July. It's found in most water beds, as well as many garden centres in recent years! Looking at the formation of the water lily, can you see how it resembles a lotus flower? (The lotus flower is the symbol of the journey of enlightenment: of emerging into the awareness of the sunlight from the muddy depths of unknowing.) Each water lily has 15–25 white petals which take their turn to unfold and finally reveal a bright, sunny centre. They are very symbolic of our own growth: each step we take in the right direction will bring us on to the next. As our inner flower unfolds, we finally reach the bright light in the centre. Unfolding each petal is not always easy, and we may fail several times, but remember, our angel is always here to pick us up, dust us down, and encourage us to take yet another step.

Hang a picture of a water lily or lotus flower in your home or workplace so that each time you see it you will remember its significance as a symbol of your spiritual development.

Don't ask yourself what the world needs.
Ask yourself what makes you come alive.
And then go out and do that ...
because what the world needs is people
who have come alive.

HAROLD WHITMAN

Why would God make the world a place of misery? There is no reason whatsoever to believe that life has to be 'a battle' or 'a vale of tears'. In fact, I feel very strongly that to believe in want and loss is to insult God. As it says in the Bible, 'ask and thou shalt receive.' So ask for joy, happiness, health and wealth. Then you can share those wonderful things with others. It is the same regarding our career and how we make money. Choose a task which you love, something which makes you feel good about yourself and about life. Then you will succeed. You cannot but succeed when you are doing things that make you feel good and things which motivate you to be happy and to smile.

Write to your angel today. Think of all the good things that have come to pass in your life, especially since you've become more aware of your angel's presence. Thank your angel for being with you through thick and thin! Make the letter as creative as possible; draw pictures, make a logo, whatever you can do to make it very, very special.

Visit a wise person today. It could be anyone, old or young. It could be a spiritual reader or an elderly neighbour. It could even be a young child, whose view of life is as yet untarnished by society's expectations. Listen to their wisdom. What can you learn from it?

The more materialistic science becomes, the more angels shall I paint. Their wings are my protest in favour of the immortality of the soul.

SIR EDWARD COLEY BURNE-JONES

You cannot change anyone but yourself. You can rail against destroyers of our ecology and our neighbourhoods, but it's up to each and every one of us to start making the changes in our own lives. I used to want to yell at people who destroyed nature, cut down trees and generally 'paved Paradise', as Joni Mitchell wrote. Nowadays I realize that if I want things to change and improve it's up to me to take the first steps. If I see someone destroying flowers or shrubs, I plant more in my garden. If I see someone cutting down a tree I take the ultimate revenge and plant two in its place!

11 July

Experience something from your childhood today. There might be a festival or fete going on that used to thrill you when you were a child. Or what about a visit to a safari park? What did you love doing as a child? Perhaps it's just eating out of doors, or sitting quietly watching the world go by! Your angel can help you to remember what it was like to relish the feeling of expectation and security that you felt when you were a child.

If we do not live, speak and think in the
language of enchantment,
including naming angels and recognising
spirits ... then the soul will go out
of our lives and communities, and we will
wonder why nothing seems to
hold together and nothing seems to have
value any more.

THOMAS MOORE, *THE RE-ENCHANTMENT OF EVERYDAY LIFE*

Look around you. What is missing in today's society? It is a sense of enchantment. The belief in possibilities. Society is a symbol of what the general public has become. Bring back enchantment into your life and you can help to bring back the soul into our society.

Ask your angel to inspire you to start a new way of thinking and living among you and your neighbours.

13 July

Be an angel today! As it's difficult for angels to manifest in human form, we can often take on their role for a moment or two and help someone in their name.

Keep your eyes – and your heart – open today. Who needs a kind word? Who needs to unburden themselves? Who needs a boost to their confidence?

Take on the role of an angel today and see how fulfilling it can be.

If we have listening ears, God speaks to us
in our own language,
whatever that language is.

MAHATMA GANDHI

Have you noticed that whether a cat or dog lives in the Philippines, the Congo, the Netherlands or California, there will be no language barrier? Yet with humans there will be. But when the language of God is being spoken, through our angels, there is no language barrier, no matter where we are living on the Planet Earth.

Symbols are international messages. They carry profound messages for everyone. Wear an angel pin on your clothes to act as a greeting to others who share your beliefs, no matter what their background. A welcoming smile costs nothing but a thought and can transform a lonely person's day. How else can you break down the language barrier? Ask your angel!

Make a pasta angel today! Yes, an angel made of pasta. It's very simple, just use whatever pasta shells you like to form the body and head of an angel: spirals, penne, macaroni ... use your imagination! Cook the pasta shells quickly in boiling water till just turned soft and allow them to cool. Then, using a needle and thread, sew them into the shape of an angel and paint or spray it in gold paint. When dry, finish off with clear varnish. Now give it a special name. You can then let this pasta angel look after plant pots, put it in your Earth Shrine ... wherever you need an angel.

16 July

Make today a special family day. Even if you live miles apart, or if some members are deceased, you can still do this ritual to come together in a loving way. Find old photographs of each member and gather keepsakes such as cards, letters, or gifts exchanged over the years.

Put each person's articles in a separate pile. Now think of each individual and choose a candle in a colour which you think would help them: red for physical energy and motivation, orange for emotional support, yellow for enthusiasm and positive attitude, green or pink for love, blue for communication and integrity, purple for spiritual awareness and white for a fresh start and purity.

Remember how each person influenced you. Even if they have hurt you, remember they didn't know any better then, and try to forgive them. As you light each candle, invite their angel to join you and send your love and light to each person as the candles burn.

Today is about play. Do you find it easy to play? If not, try to spend at least part of today with a child or children. Watch how uncritical they are; see how carefree they are. Remember, you were once like that, so allow yourself to be like a child again. (If you find this difficult, ask Archangel Gabriel, who looks after our creative and expressive energy, to help you to remember.) Laugh for the sake of laughing! Even if it's the last thing you feel like today, begin with a simple 'Ha, ha, ha!' And repeat it in different tones. This can end up as great fun if you do it with others! Try something new. It doesn't matter if it doesn't work, just try it!

Light an orange candle and as you watch it burn imagine in your mind's eye an image of yourself with a light heart and laughing with joy!

Prepare for a miracle!

ANGEL INSPIRATION

Sometimes we lose faith and become so low that we simply cannot imagine that our lives can change for the better, we cannot believe that a miracle can happen. 'Prepare for a miracle!' was a message that I received some years ago from my own angel, when my thinking was negative and when I believed only in struggle and lack. I wrote it down in the exact way that it came to me, and I wondered why I had been given that message. After some thought I hit on the word 'prepare'. I needed to 'prepare', to 'make ready', for I had at that point forgotten that miracles could happen. I was so low that if a miracle had been offered to me on the street I would have walked straight by it, believing it was for someone else! It's so easy to lose faith and so lose our way. We all need to discard those negative beliefs and, instead, prepare for a better way, for a better life.

19 July

During the First World War (1914–1918), in a town on the Belgian/French border, the Allies had only two regiments remaining and were outnumbered 100–1 by the Germans.

Then a bright being 'with yellow hair and golden armour and riding on a white horse' came to their aid, 'looking for all the world like St. George, the patron saint of England', said the British soldiers. Archangel Michael's light shone on what looked like thousands of British troops lying in position against the German army. The German horses refused to move forward, and they turned sharply and fled. It was a turning point in the Battle of Mons. This story has been related by many soldiers on both the Allied and German sides.

Often we fear ridicule if we speak of our own angel experiences. But remember, your gentle messages of angels may make a huge difference to just one person. And then you'll know you've made a worthwhile difference.

20 July

Do something different today. It doesn't matter what the weather is like, how much money you have or don't have, who you share your life with and how many, today you must promise yourself to try something different to the norm!

It's all about breaking free of the daily routine we tend to fall into. It's about opening up to new possibilities and making a new 'blueprint' to follow for a new life. Travel to work a different way. Have lunch at 9 am and breakfast at 4 pm. See a movie straight after work. Go for a walk during your lunch break. Sing as you work, dance as you walk ...! Use your imagination and ask the angels to inspire you!

Then, as you go to bed, think back on the pattern you have just broken and the new one you can now follow.

When we are judging ourself or others we cannot connect with our angel because they communicate through the energy of love. If we are holding issues of unforgiveness in our heart it's virtually impossible to hear their messages. Sometimes we need to have a 'breakdown' when we feel most vulnerable in order to have a 'breakthrough'. We must first go through the fear and anger before we can feel it and let it go. From then on we can purify our hearts and so allow our angel's love and messages to come in.

Are you holding judgement or unforgiveness in your heart? Say aloud, *'The Angel of Divine Forgiveness goes before me and prepares my way'* whenever you remember something you need to feel and let go of.

There are only two ways to live your life.
One is as though nothing is a miracle.
The other is as though everything is a miracle.

ALBERT EINSTEIN

No matter how your life seems to be going at present, celebrate the miracle of life. That every day and every night, no matter how bad they seem, die away. And the next day and the next night is a new time altogether. Everything is possible on that day, especially when you are aware of your angel's presence and comforting help. Look in the mirror and say, *'Today is a new day and I am a new me.'*

The Sun moves into the Fire sign of Leo today, which is governed by the Sun itself. Archangel Raphael looks after this month, so wear something bright and fiery today! Choose orange, ochre, peach … it will draw Raphael's 'go get it!' energy to you and help you be more expressive. This is a good month for social gatherings and family get-togethers.

Ask Archangel Raphael to help you bring joy and creativity into your life. Light a yellow or orange candle to celebrate this archangel's presence with us all for the next four weeks.

24 July

Angels look for an opening in our consciousness,
then they slip into our thoughts ... our dreams.

LINDA GEORGIAN

Angels come to us in our dreams if we cannot and will not
accept them in our waking hours.

We need to remember the importance of our dream messages. They come to us from the world of spirit, whether it's
from our angels, our spirit guides or our own 'higher self'.
Dream messages are usually shown to us in symbols. Write
down everything you see or hear in your dreams. Think
about the meaning of these things. What's happening in your
life at the moment, and how could your dream symbols relate
to it? Don't ignore your dreams. They give us guidance and
the ability to contact a little piece of Heaven every time we
sleep, even though we are currently stuck firmly on the
Earth. Remember to ask your angels to appear to you in your
dreams if you hesitate to contact them when you are awake!

Many times in my past I have been hugely disappointed because I got turned down for a job or because something I'd been expecting hadn't turned out as I'd planned. It's only with hindsight that I've understood why this obstacle has happened.

Think back on the major disappointments you have had in the past few years. Now make a list of all those disappointments on the left side of a sheet of paper. Then sit quietly and ask your angel to help you remember what it was that happened instead? As you record this on the right side of the page, can you begin to see how you ended up with a better outcome than you had first awaited?

This is proof that the angels give us 'the perfect outcome' for us at that time. They do know better than us what we deserve, and we so often undersell ourselves! When you feel uncertain as to what you want to happen in your life, ask for 'the perfect outcome', and that's exactly what the angels will synchronize for you!

I am ever under the gaze of an angel who
protects and prays for me.

POPE JOHN XXIII

Look on your angel as your dearest, closest friend. Someone who never discards you, someone who is always there, no matter whether it's day or night, no matter what the time. Treat your angel as your friend, a friend who knows what is right and is always willing to offer you the correct path to follow.

27 July

The films *City of Angels* and *The Preacher's Wife* make the following very strong points about our interaction with angels.

1. Angels are here to give us guidance.

And ...

2. They cannot make us take it!

Angels are sent here to guide us through our lives. They are not here to force us into any action; if they were we would never have to learn anything, and that wouldn't be the point of life at all. So no matter who we are or where we live, we have one thing in common, and that is free will. We can ask for guidance and we can reject it. That's our choice. Because angels are here to guide us, we must first ask them for guidance. So how do you ask? You ask just as you would ask a friend for help, such as *'Angel, could you help work this problem out for me?'* Once you ask, you'll be surprised just how quickly the help comes to you. (And do remember to say 'thanks'!)

Love allows a person to see the true angelic nature
of another person, the halo, the aureole of divinity.

THOMAS MOORE

When we 'fall in love' we see 'the perfect divine essence' of someone. That is, what they can become. However, most people are not aware of their divinity, their ability to connect with God through their angels and so reach and fulfil their higher path. Because of this, they tend to stumble and fall, and then we may sit in judgement because they did so! It's vital to understand that everyone is doing the best they can under the circumstances as they see them. It's imperative to understand that we, too, are doing the best we can. See the best in yourself and others, but try not to sit in judgement if anyone should fail to attain their highest aspiration. To err is human, to forgive divine!

I give workshops on dream interpretation, and quite often people will say 'I never, ever dream!' But they must dream, we all do. As Shakespeare wrote in Hamlet, 'To sleep, perchance to dream ...' We sleep in order to dream, so that we can connect with our spiritual self, otherwise we would end up quite literally going insane!

To help you remember your dreams, keep amethyst crystal or herkimer diamond by your bed. Have marigold flowers nearby – crush a couple of petals in your fingers and breathe in their scent – or put a drop of marigold essence on your pillow. These will help you more easily connect with your dreaming self and so accept the symbolic messages you are conveyed in dreams while you sleep.

As I mentioned before, sometimes we may fear a meeting with an angel in the daylight hours, and if this is so, ask your angel to come to you in your dreams. An angelic dream is very vivid, especially in colour, and not easily forgotten!

As the month of July draws to a close, in what ways is your life more balanced now with the help of this month's angel, Verchiel? If you took Angel Verchiel's advice you will now have more time for both work and play, and you'll find that the better balanced you are in your own life, the better your bank account balance becomes! What changes have you already made, and what do you plan to change over the coming weeks? Thank Angel Verchiel for its help in assisting you to find a happy balance in your life.

Today is the Celtic festival of Lughnasa, which gets its name from Lugh, the Sun God, and at this time our pastoral ancestors would celebrate the first harvest of grain, whether it was wheat or barley. It would have been marked by some form of ritual, such as dressing up as Straw Men or taking the part of the Corn King, all of these ceremonies being played out in order to please the God of the Sun, so that he would bring the light and warmth back to the land the next growing season.

Hold a special ceremony today, perhaps a simple picnic, and thank the Celtic Angel of the North for helping us to bring in an abundant harvest and ensuring our wellbeing and protection. Invite this angel back into our lives again when the pastoral year turns once more so that we can all be assured of healthy stock and filled store cupboards!

The Angel of August

Hamaliel

(Southern Hemisphere - Hamaliel is the Angel of February)

1 August

Now that our harvest is assured we need to remember to thank the soil, the devas and all the other micro-systems of nature which have helped bring the gardens and fields to this abundant time. Often we take for granted some of the gifts we've been given. In order to make the most of what we have in our homes, our family, our career and our environment, we must not turn away from the need to tend carefully what we have begun. Hamaliel, the Angel of August, will help us maintain our stamina when we need to put extra effort into our lives. Wear green or olive colours to encourage other types of abundance into your life – an abundance of love, support, health, wealth and wisdom!

In order to honour the growing harvest, why not sprinkle some little 'crystal seeds' or some 'angel, stars and moon confetti' around your garden?

2 August

The crystal for August is peridot, a green coloured crystal which can vary from yellow-green to bottle-green. Ever heard the saying 'green with envy'? Wearing this crystal can help you leave those feelings of inadequacy behind and help you to strengthen your own feelings of self-worth. These crystals are quite abundant, so they are easily found as tumble stones or in jewellery.

Wear this crystal close to your heart and remember that, no matter how lowly you may feel in comparison to others on occasion, we're all equal in the eyes of God, and each and every one of us has our angel!

One can never consent to creep
when one feels an impulse to soar.

HELEN KELLER

If you are the only person within your group who has opened up to spiritual development, it is often difficult to come into the open and express your new-found feelings of freedom and the excitement of a growing inner knowledge. Try not to allow other people's opinions of you to hold you back. Everyone is on a path of spiritual development, it's just that some are travelling at a different pace than others. Ask your angel to guide you to meet like-minded people so that you can discuss and exchange ideas and information that will help you soar above everyday problems every now and again!

4 August

For an angel of peace, a faithful guide,
a guardian of our souls and bodies,
let us entreat the Lord.
LITURGY OF THE EASTERN ORTHODOX CHURCH

Practically every belief system or religion, whether from the West or the East, includes beings – called angels, peri, fravashi or devas – who are sent by God to undertake special missions with us humans here on Earth. It is because they are the intermediaries between ourselves and the Source (God) that they can work magic with us.

Make a special effort today to talk with your angel and thank it for its presence in your life. Imagine a conversation in your mind, or even speak aloud if you wish. Chat about your daily tasks and your family and friends. Chat as though you can actually see your angel beside you, just as you would a friend or even a pet! Angels want us to be 'buddies', not separate from them. How can they possibly help bring magic into our lives unless we are open and accepting of them?

The poppy is the flower of August. Look around you in fields, gardens and building sites and you'll see the wonderful poppy growing there regardless of the soil, regardless of neglect. The seeds lie in the soil for many years and will keep germinating and showing their bright, cheerful faces to the Sun.

The poppy grew abundantly on the soil of the Somme and other battlefields of World War 1, and has since come to symbolize those lost in war. Today, think of those lost in battles all over the globe and those grieving for them. Think of the futility of manifesting our fears through warlike behaviour. Whenever you see a poppy, send a thought of love through your angel to the angels of those who are living in fear. Ask your angel to help their angels shower more love than ever into those people's fear-filled hearts.

Be patient. All will be revealed in 'Angel Time'.

ANGEL INSPIRATION

Possibly one of the most difficult things to learn is patience, especially when you are teetering on a tightrope between faith and failure! But this is something we all do need to learn. The angels know better than us, and we have to accept that. When we ask for something we will get it, but when? Life is a process. What you do today will have an effect on the next step you take. If you keep wanting to leapfrog over the learning process you will never learn what you are here to learn, you will never experience all that you need to experience.

When you ask the angels for help, believe without exception that help is on its way. But do remember, the changes in your life will come about at the time that is right for you, what is known as 'Angel Time'.

Do you ever discuss matters of 'life and death' with your friends and family? Do your children ever ask you questions about angels, death or birth? If so, do you dismiss them or encourage them to question? There are many books available which have researched 'near-death experiences' during which many people, young and old, religious and non-religious, have had wonderful spiritual visions. Firstly, they tend to leave their body and see it beneath them as they lift free of their physical presence. Then what they term 'a Light' or 'a Light Being' comes to them and leads them on a journey during which time they often go back through earlier experiences and review what occurred. At some point they are given the chance to return to their body or to stay in 'heaven'. These experiences are always recorded as being life changing, giving the person more insight into their own purpose in life.

What life changing experiences have you had? How have they changed you? What are your priorities now? Spend today thinking about these questions.

We shall find peace. We shall hear the angels.
We shall see the sky sparkling with diamonds.

ANTON CHEKHOV

Close your eyes tonight when you are lying in bed, ready for sleep. Imagine in your mind's eye that you are opening a window in the ceiling of your bedroom and there, above you, is the most magnificent sight ... an inky black sky with hundreds of thousands of stars shining and sparkling out of the darkness. Now imagine you can see angels winging their way from star to star across the sky. Who knows, perhaps a 'shooting star' is really a band of angels on their nightly journey through the stars?

Here's a fun activity for young and old: Salt Dough Angels. Why not encourage your children to make these as gifts? They're easy to make and cost very little, and more than likely you already have the required ingredients in your kitchen.

You will need:

    475 g/1 lb plain flour
    475 g/1 lb table salt
    200 ml/7 fl oz warm water

For decoration: food colour or powder paints, craft glue, acrylic paint and clear varnish.

Make a stiff, workable dough by mixing together the flour and salt and adding the warm water gradually. If you wish to colour your dough, divide it into smaller portions and add food colour or dry paint powder. (Otherwise, leave till dry and use acrylic paint, as directed below.) As you roll out the 'pastry' to about ½ cm/¼ inch in thickness make sure there's no cracks or air bubbles, then cut into the shapes you require.

(You can use the templates on page 34 for angel designs, or invent your own!) Join the pieces together into an angel shape with the aid of a fork, and add decorations such as curly hair, a halo on top of her hair, stars or moons in her hands or on her clothes. You can also insert any design into her clothing with a fork or skewer. Attach a small hanger of some sort on the back (such as those you'd use for a net curtain) or a paper clip.

You can now leave this to dry for a few days or bake on a flat tray in the oven at 200°C/400°F/Gas Mark 5 for 3–4 hours. When dry, paint on a thin coat of craft glue as a sealant. When this has dried, paint and decorate with acrylic paints. Finally, seal your Salt Dough Angels with one coat of clear varnish.

10 August

Walk around your locality and take a deeper look at your surroundings. How many churches depict angels in their windows or their architecture? How many shops have angels in their displays? How many parks have angel statues? Have fun noticing what's going on in your locality. You're sure to discover lots of symbols of angels clearly on display for everyone to see. If you do this with someone else, make it into a fun competition!

Robert Holden's book, *Laughter, the Best Medicine*, proves through scientific study that laughter releases healing hormones into the bloodstream and so helps to heal all sorts of diseases. There are several 'Laughter Clinics' in the UK offering people this special therapy which, for some reason, we have forgotten is free to us all!

I feel that the day I learned to laugh at myself was the day I began to start my healing process. By doing this we can get balance back into our lives, we can stop judging ourselves and learn to live more easily with others. When did you first laugh at yourself? When did you last laugh, period?

Today learn to laugh again. It's simple, especially when you know you have your angel to help you. Even if you're feeling miserable it can work! Say aloud 'Ha, ha, ha!' Now repeat it: 'Ha, ha, ha!' Repeat it again, and again ... Before long you'll find your face is breaking into a grin and you cannot help yourself, you just have to laugh! It's even more fun when you do this exercise with others.

12 August

The angels share with no strings attached.

TERRY LYNN TAYLOR AND MARY BETH CRAIN,

ANGEL WISDOM

There's an old saying from the world of commerce, 'There's no such thing as a free lunch'; in other words, you get nothing for nothing. That's not always true, at least not when it comes to angels! For angels will give us love, protection, understanding, compassion and all those things which are essential to our wellbeing, and ask for absolutely nothing in return. You don't have to be anywhere near perfect, be religious, be a 'do-gooder' or even be smart, you still have your angel every moment of every day. This is the one and only relationship you can enjoy where there really are no strings attached.

Invite the Angel of Surrender into your life today. Don't worry, it doesn't mean you give up your newly found self-empowerment! 'Surrender' is just about acknowledging that your angel really does know best and, rather than fight against what deep inside you know is right, you give in to the higher power of God and the angels.

Remember we're all here at this 'University of Life' in order to learn. If we see the angels as our 'professors' then we can understand why we sometimes need to surrender to their greater knowledge. But it's not about throwing in the towel. It's about saying, 'I know you know better than me. Please help me release my need for control. I surrender to you.' By letting go we actually free ourselves from the problem we've created for ourselves, that of a lack of faith.

The angel of the Lord said to me in a dream 'Jacob!'
And I said 'Here I am, Lord.'

GENESIS 31:11, THE BIBLE

Incubate your dreams. Dreams are messages from your spirit and often our angels can appear in them.

Before you go to sleep tonight, ask your angel to help you to have a helpful and memorable dream to give you guidance about what to do, and when to do it. Keep a pad and pen very close to your bed so that, on awakening, you are ready to jot down the main elements of your dream. How did you feel in the dream? Did you see any familiar faces? Where were you? Who was with you? What happened? What does that dream mean to you? The more you record your dream messages, the easier it will be to understand them.

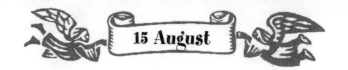

Bring good fortune into your life with this simple ritual. Find a gold, yellow or orange candle, then add the following to a small bottle of grapeseed oil and shake gently:

    8 drops frankincense essential oil

    8 drops lemon essential oil

    16 drops lavender essential oil

    1 drop citronella essential oil

    some saffron threads (or marigold petals)

Pour some into your hands and massage the candle. Start in the middle and anoint it downwards (towards Mother Earth), then from the middle upwards (towards heaven). Light the candle and ask your angel to help you attract good things into your life.

You can also anoint any special item such as an angel figure or special charm which you can carry with you to bring good fortune.

We are born to walk with angels but, instead, we search for jewels in the mud.

ANGEL INSPIRATION

Being human beings we tend to place more emphasis on physical things: possessions, money, our body ... When life seems to have taken a wrong turning we tend to seek more things to own, a better body, an updated model of a car, a bigger home, and so on. But the answer does not lie in physical fulfilment. It lies in knowing that we are here with a purpose and that we are fulfilling that purpose. That's what's known as 'spiritual fulfilment', knowing you're doing something that makes a difference. When we are facing moments of uncertainty, when we feel a sense of emptiness, we must connect with our angels in order to understand our true purpose in life, rather than try to fill the empty void with possession after possession.

Make some angelica tea today. It tastes similar to China tea. You can use the dried variety (if so, one teaspoon per person), but if you are growing the herb angelica itself, the taste will be fresher and richer. As the leaves are large, it's rather difficult to give exact measures, but generally one leaf per person is a good guide. Warm a teapot first, then gently crush the leaf or leaves and pour boiling water over them. Let them steep for no longer than 10 minutes, strain and serve.

Angelica tea is served hot and is very good for a healthy digestion.

Carry out the following ritual when you are really committed to having something in your life. It involves connecting with the angels of the Four Directions: North, South, East and West. (If you don't know which direction is which, ask yourself, where does the Sun rise in the morning? That is east. Face that way now. Behind you is west, to your left is the north and to your right is the south.)

Carry out this ritual out of doors. Take some bay leaves, crush them in your hands and divide them into four portions.

Stand facing north, and blow just a quarter of the bay leaves towards the north, and say:

> *Angel of the North, please take with you to the*
> *northern direction*
> *my request to bring me success in this venture.*

Now stand facing east, and blow a quarter of the bay leaves towards the east, and say:

*Angel of the East, please take with you to the easterly
direction my request to bring me success in this venture.*

Now stand facing south, and blowing a quarter of the bay
leaves towards the south, say:

*Angel of the South, please take with you to
the southerly direction
my request to bring me success in this venture.*

Now stand facing west, and blowing the remainder of the bay
leaves towards the west, say:

*Angel of the West, please take with you to the
westerly direction
my request to bring me success in this venture.*

When this is done, thank the angels for their help and leave
them to get on with the task. Do not ask again; trust that it is
in hand.

19 August

Become aware today. So often our days seem to go by in a whirl of activity and distraction. We are so busy we cannot even remember what we achieved! Stop and slow down today. Be aware of everything: your skin, your hair, your shoes, the food you eat, the flowers you see, the breeze against your face.

The more aware you become of each and every moment, the more aware you will be of angelic presence. Does the energy around you change from warm to cold? Do you feel someone is close by yet when you turn around there's nobody there? Be aware. Savour every moment of today!

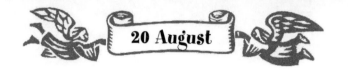

We cannot part with our friends.
We cannot let our angels go.
We do not see that they only go out
That archangels may come in.

RALPH WALDO EMERSON

It's perfectly human to fear change and, above all, a sense of emptiness within. Yet in order to learn and grow we must be willing to let go, to free ourselves from things and people who are no longer good for us. It is only when we have created that space, that vacuum, that change for the better can begin to enter our lives.

Spend a few minutes today studying a tree in detail. Note its trunk. How tall or broad is it? What pattern can you see on its bark? Are the branches sturdy or graceful? What shape and colour are the leaves? Can you see any wildlife living in it? What birds make their home there?

As you stand close to the tree try to feel, or hear, the angelic beings close by who are working in collaboration with nature. Say aloud, or in your mind, *'Hail be, unto thee, oh good living tree and all who live on it, made by the creator!'* Thank the devic beings for their daily help and energy. The more you do so, the closer they will feel to you.

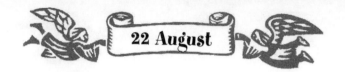

Celebrate the fruits of the summer.

Invite your angel to share a meal with you today. Use as many fresh vegetables, fruit and herbs as you can, preferably organic where possible. Don't just eat your meal, taste it and savour its freshness and life-giving nutrients.

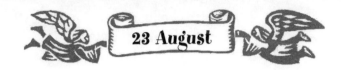

23 August

The Sun moves into the zodiac sign of Virgo today. This is an Earth Sign, symbolizing the Virgin, a sign of purity and perfection. Virgoans tend to look after 'the nitty gritty', but can be so perfectionist that they fear trying anything new in case they don't succeed!

Archangel Michael looks after this sign. He is often seen with a sword in his hand, slaying the dragon. 'The dragon' symbolizes our fears. When we ask Archangel Michael to help us he will, but we must be willing to look at our fears which, as stated before, exist only in our mind.

Whatever your zodiac sign, wear orange, white or gold over the next four weeks. They will help attract to you the best aspects of Virgoans, including the ability to see the finer details of life! Light candles of the same colour and, as you look into the flame, know that you will be given the gifts of motivation and communication.

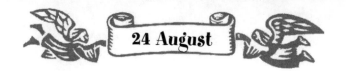

The Lord shall send his angel with you
and make your journey successful.

GENESIS 24:40, THE BIBLE

Several years ago I was driving through a rather neglected area of Dublin when I got stuck at traffic lights with a large refuse collection unit in front of me and a big construction lorry behind. Fortunately I had remembered that morning to clear up my passenger seat and I'd invited my angel to travel with me as I drove, for as I waited for the traffic lights to change two young boys came running towards my car and made to smash my passenger window. I watched with dread and could almost hear the intake of breath of those other drivers who were looking on! Even though I had little to steal, a smashed window would need repair and this was during the time when I was severely 'financially challenged'. Just centimetres from the window the two young boys came to a startling halt, a look of shock and terror crossed their faces, and they raced back where they'd come from without doing any damage to me or my car. What had they seen that made them stop and run? I firmly believe my angel manifested something or some person in the passenger seat at that very last moment to help me!

When you're travelling, make sure to consciously invite your angel along with you. Clear up a seat in the car, make room on the bus, train or plane. The more aware you are that you have a companion beside you, the more likely your journey will end happily. Encourage children to do the same, and the angel's presence can help prevent those siblings bickering as an added bonus!

Are you having difficulties with anyone in particular? Do you find that the general public are unhelpful? Do you feel unsupported by friends and family?

You can begin to heal these issues in your life by doing the following: try to understand that the 'problem' is really a 'lesson' you need to learn. Can you try to look on it as a 'lesson' just for a moment or two? Is it possible that the person causing you trouble is going to prove to be a 'blessing in disguise' in the long run? Believe it or not, it can often be those who cause us most trouble that help us the most! They force us to make changes in our lives which get us out of a 'stuck' position and get us moving!

Today make a special effort to look on any areas of trouble in your life as though you are seeing it with a bird's eye view. If you were a stranger coming across that 'problem', what would you see? Is it possible that there is another way to sort out the problem in a gentle, compassionate way? Ask your angel for insight. Then listen to the guidance!

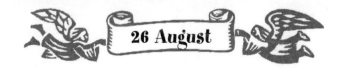

Let your life be like Angel Food Cake ...
sweet and light.

ANON

There's nothing quite as sweet and light as this delicious cake: Chocolate Angel Food Cake. It will be even lighter and more scrumptious if you invite your angel to help you make it.

You will need:

   1 tablespoon cocoa
   340 g/12 oz granulated sugar
   115 g/4 oz self-raising flour
   3–4 egg whites
   ¼ teaspoon cream of tartar
   pinch of salt
   1 teaspoon vanilla essence
   1 teaspoon almond essence (optional)
   castor sugar to sprinkle on top
   fresh fruit for topping, such as kiwis, raspberries or strawberries

Pre-heat the oven to 175°C/350°F/Gas Mark 4.

Firstly, sift the cocoa with 225 g/8 oz of sugar into a bowl and leave aside. Into a separate bowl, sift the flour three times with the remaining sugar. Separately, whisk the egg whites until foamy, then add salt and cream of tartar, and then whisk until they form stiff peaks. Now fold the egg whites into the cocoa mixture. Then fold the flour mixture into this cocoa mixture. Blend in the vanilla and/or almond essence.

Pour the mixture into a standard-size greased cake or flan tin and bake for approximately 40 minutes. Take out of the oven and invert the cake in its tin on a rack until it is cool. This will allow it to remain light and retain its volume. Then loosen the sides with a knife and turn onto a serving plate. Sprinkle with castor sugar and/or top off with fresh fruit such as kiwi, raspberries or strawberries.

27 August

A guardian angel o'er his life presiding,
Doubling his pleasures, and his cares dividing.

SAMUEL ROGERS

Be aware. Awareness is essential if we are to be open to angelic help. So often we can allow each moment of each hour to blend into one with nothing to distinguish one day from the next. Being aware that your angel is here with you at this moment can bring about a renaissance in your daily life. Look at the dewdrops. Look at the rainbow. Watch a bird in flight. See the joy in a child's eyes. Look with your eyes and your heart. Be aware! No second can be taken back, no second repeated. Every moment is a special moment with your angel at your side.

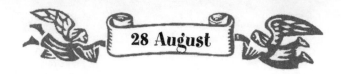

This is a time when students start the new academic year at school. When your child is setting off for school each morning, ask that *'The Angel of Divine Protection goes before* .... *[name] and prepares his/her way.'* You may also like to have a little container by your front door holding some sort of angel cards (perhaps the Angel Inspiration cards that you have made yourself from this book, as suggested on 5 July, or you could choose a set from the many varieties on sale in retail outlets). Encourage your child to take an angel message before leaving the house in the morning. Get into the habit of it yourself!

Your voice is my voice.
(Speak up on behalf of your angel.)

ANGEL INSPIRATION

When I first began giving my 'Talking with Angels' workshops back in the mid-90's, I sometimes wondered if I was a spokesperson for the angels or if I was just having an ego trip! One night I awoke hearing the above message clearly in my ear. I took it as a positive sign! Sometimes we can be the spokesperson for our angels; just ask what to say and you will hear your voice saying it.

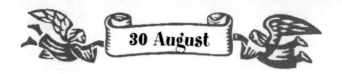

How are your finances going along at the moment? Are your outgoings out of balance with your income? There's a simple step you can take to get the angels to help you balance your books.

Get all your bills together, with the highest amount at the bottom of the pile. Now get a big envelope and put all your bills into it. Write on the front of the envelope the words 'proof of my credibility'. Then place a symbol of an angel (a figure, a picture, a drawing) on top of the envelope and leave it somewhere safe for ten days. By that time the angels should have helped you to see that these 'bills' are actually proof that you are a person of credibility, someone who can be trusted to use utilities in advance without paying because your creditors know you better than you know yourself! Often the 'help' the angels can give you is the ability to contact your creditors and rearrange your payments, or to get a helpful hand from your bank manager.

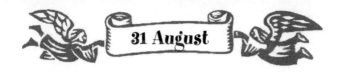

Thank the Angel of August, Hamaliel, for all the abundance of your current harvest. Look out for Harvest Festivals and other meetings of Thanksgiving. If there isn't one in your area, why not arrange one yourself? Either hold one just for your family (or you and your angel), or else extend invitations to other like-minded people. Ask everyone to bring some symbol of this year's harvest to date: fruit, vegetables, a sheaf of corn ... whatever you feel is abundant in your life.

Light green candles if possible to honour Angel Hamaliel and make a nice ceremony of celebration together. If you're doing this on a large scale, make up baskets of your harvest and share it with those less fortunate in your community. You might also like to donate some money to a charity of your choosing so that your abundance can be shared with others, no matter how many miles might separate you.

The Angel of September

Uriel

(Southern Hemisphere - Uriel is the Angel of March)

This is the month to harvest what we have planted and tend-ed. Some things we worked on begin to die away now, and we may be reluctant to let things go. Archangel Uriel, the Angel of September, helps us see the cyclical nature of life, growth and death.

Give thanks to Uriel, who looks after this planet, for the air we breathe and the food we eat.

As you prepare or enjoy food today, take a few moments to bless the food on your plate. It's a nice idea to light a candle as you eat your food, helping you to be more aware of the importance of this commodity in your life, and reminding you that we are part of the Earth and everything that grows on it, rather than apart from it.

As students young and old prepare for the new school and college term, the excitement of learning is in the air around us.

Whether in your own home, a library or a bookshop, pick up a book at random. Close your eyes and ask the Angel of Learning to be with you now to help you find out what you need to know today. Allow your inner knowing to help you open the right page. Now let your fingers move along the page and, when it feels right, stop and open your eyes and read what's written there. What did you discover? What do you need to learn?

Angels know your good bits and your bad bits,
and they still love you.

ANGEL INSPIRATION

How close do you feel right now to your angel? If you are finding it difficult to connect it is because you are holding back. Are you judging yourself and therefore stopping yourself from enjoying their love and support?

As already stated, no-one is perfect, nor are we meant to be perfect. We are all here at this 'University of Life' to learn lessons specific to our needs. Like a loving parent, our angel wants only good for us. However, they know we have free will and so cannot force us to go one way or the other. Forgive yourself now for being imperfect, and open your heart to your angel's support.

September's crystal is Sapphire, usually blue in colour. The three points of a star sapphire signify Body, Mind and Spirit. The bodily needs include food, clothes, sex, home, money, affection...; the mind requires the knowledge, intellect and philosophies by which we live; while the spiritual needs are unique to each of us: it could be looking after environmental issues, being president of a country, running a business, looking after the less able, or working in the healing/holistic professions. Whatever makes you feel fulfilled is right for you.

What are you doing to ensure the happy balance between Body, Mind and Spirit? Find a blue crystal (sapphire is often priced out of our reach) and contemplate your priorities in life. Do you feel a person of worth, even if you don't get paid for what you do? Or do you feel, no matter how much you are paid, that your life is not worthwhile? Only you can answer these questions. Be truthful to yourself. Choose a path which is fulfilling to your inner being.

We trust in plumed procession
For such the angels go –
Rank after rank, with even feet
And uniforms of snow.

EMILY DICKINSON

Have a bit of fun today by making up some angel rhymes and poems. They can be humorous. They can be esoteric in nature. Whatever seems right for you, follow that muse! If you can encourage your friends and family to join you in this creative pursuit, all the better!

If you have a garden, or even a patio, check your local garden centre for the beautiful, sweet-scented angel white lilac bush, Angel White (botanical name, *Syringa vulgaris*).

Now is a very good time to plant trees and shrubs. The Angel White lilac is excellent for warm winter areas. It grows spectacular clusters of fragrant pure white flowers without winter chilling! It has an open-branched, upright form which can be used as a hedge, screen or to draw the viewer's eyes to a particular spot in the garden. This is a deciduous shrub, which needs full to partial sun. It's a fast grower, reaching a height of 3.7 m/12 ft and a spread of 3m/10 ft, so make sure you have enough space for it!

God sends forth the angels as His messengers,
with two, three or four pairs of wings.

THE KORAN

As you know, you don't have to follow any religion or belong to one religion in order to have angels, for angels were created by God while religions were created by mankind. I find religions fascinating. There are so many, some which differ dramatically, others which have just a small amount of disagreement. It's sad to see how religious belief can divide so many people when, in the end, they are meant to bring people together under the one umbrella, the one God.

What do you know about other people's religion? Do you ever discuss it? What about going onto the internet and checking up on the history and development of your own religion if you follow one, and then on other religions?

It's vital that each of us remembers that we are responsible for our actions. Everything we do has a re-action. By taking extra care of how we treat our own 'back yard', whether it's a farm, a garden, a balcony or a window box, we can work along with Archangel Uriel and become more aware of the health of our environment.

If you go shopping today take special note of your purchases. How much packaging are you bringing home with you? How do you dispose of it? Can you recycle any of it? Is there any way you can buy goods without unnecessary packaging? Give Uriel a helping hand today!

As the seasons change it's time to think about next year's garden. Remember the more abundant your garden, the more devic beings can live there and share their gifts with you!

It's always a good idea to see the flower, shrub or tree in reality so that you can tell if it would suit your space. So take a trip to a garden centre or nursery and see what plants you might like to have in your garden or flower pot.

What about the climber 'Angel Wing' jasmine (*Jasminium nitidum*), or 'Blue Angel' clematis (*Clematis viticella*) which has sky blue flowers from June to September? If you have the space, look out for Japanese angelica, also known as *Aralia*, reaching 4 m/13 ft in height, with branches spanning the same width. Rose lovers might look for 'Smooth Angel', a thornless hybrid tea-rose or 'Angel Face' floribunda.

There's plenty of time to seek these out in specialist stockists if needs be. (More suggestions follow later in the month.)

10 September

Be an angel to someone today! It won't cost you anything but a thought! Invite someone to share their troubles with you. Greet someone who looks lonely. Help a stranger who seems lost. Ask your angel to join their angel today to give a troubled person some extra care and attention. Know that you have made a difference today!

Four-year-old Juliana McCourt believed in angels. Her Grandma and she knew that every time they found a thread in an unexpected place it was a gift from their angels reminding them that they were somewhere around. Juliana brightened up everyone's life, especially her parents who had met in their later years and hadn't expected to have any children, let alone such a charming little one as Juliana! Then on 11 September 2001, she and her mum boarded a plane which was deliberately crashed into the Twin Towers in New York. Her mum's best friend was in the second plane that hit the Towers, and her Uncle Ron was in one of the Towers itself when the event happened, but he escaped miraculously.

Several days after the incident her anguished grandma was facing another day of heartbreak. Distraught, she asked God for some sign that there was a reason to go on living. She sat at her dressing table as she did every day and, as usual, picked up a jar of face cream. Suddenly her heart raced, she could hardly believe what she saw: there, under the jar, was a bunch of threads waiting to be found by her. The message clearly was 'I'm still around you, the angels are still around you.' This small yet momentous sign from the spirit world helped to begin to heal many broken hearts.

What little things do you do every day, little things that you share with those you love? Sometimes we're too busy to recognize the power of these rituals that we share with one another. Yet in our darkest hours they can be the tower of strength that we cling on to to keep our sanity. Be aware of them today: the family jokes that only you understand, the sayings that mean so much to you, yet are just words to others ...be aware and be grateful for those special, secret things you share with love.

*Within each of our spirits there is our Self
and many Angels.*

ANGEL INSPIRATION

I believe everyone is a spirit which is enveloped by a human form. What we see as human beings is each person's physical, human expression. Yet we are much more than that. For within our spirit there is the ego, the conscious self, and the connection with many angels. It's our ego that is the fearful part of us. Try not to fight it. Instead, treat it as a little frightened child. Console it and let your angels surround it with love and understanding. Then you can move forward into change and enlightenment more freely and easily.

Next time you feel too afraid to take a step in the right direction, stand back and imagine you can see yourself as though you are a little child standing at the edge of the pavement, wanting to cross the road but too frightened to take the next step. Imagine now that your angel comes to you, takes your hand and gently but firmly leads you across that road.

13 September

Are devoutly religious people also believers in UFOs, ESP and psychic ability? The January/February 2000 issue of *Skeptical Inquirer, The Magazine for Science and Reason*, indicates that the two belief systems often go hand-in-hand.

Erich Goode, Professor of Sociology at the State University of New York at Stony Brook, surveyed almost 500 students, asking them dozens of questions pertaining to religious and paranormal beliefs. Goode's response to the results is: 'There may only be a hair's breadth separating belief in angels from belief in ghosts, belief in the curative power of Lourdes from belief in psychic surgery, and belief in heaven from belief that UFOs are not only real but piloted by superhuman beings.'

An angel's presence can't be proved scientifically, it can only be proved with hindsight. That's where faith comes in. You can't buy it, you can't bottle it, you can only develop it in your own life with your own experiences. Develop faith in your angels today.

Here's a fun recipe for Sesame Halos, which are quick and easy to make. With a little adult supervision, children can enjoy making them, too.

For 12–15 Sesame Halos you will need:
- 50 g/2 oz sesame seeds (toasted till golden brown)
- 225 g/8 oz dark brown sugar
- 225 g/8 oz white granulated sugar
- 250 ml/8 fl oz single cream
- 2 tablespoons butter
- 225 g/8 oz pecan nuts (halved)

To toast the sesame seeds, preheat the oven to 180°C/350°F/Gas Mark 4, and place the seeds on a tray in the oven for 10–12 minutes until golden brown.

Now place the dark brown and white sugar in a saucepan and add the cream. Heat gently until the sugar dissolves, and then bring the mixture to the boil until it reaches 105°C /221°F.

(Check the temperature with a cooking thermometer.) Now add the butter, pecan nuts and sesame seeds. Continue stirring occasionally until the mixture has reached 106°C /223°F on the cooking thermometer, the 'soft ball' stage. Remove from the heat and cool for a couple of minutes, then stir again until it has thickened. Then, using a dessert spoon, drop the mixture onto buttered foil or a tray and quickly form into 12–15 halo shapes. Voila! These are your Sesame Halos.

Communication is vital for happy relationships, yet quite often it is the very component which breaks down.

If you are having a problem with a friend or close family member and find it difficult to communicate with them about how you feel, ask your angel to speak to your friend's angel. Ask that when you are in contact with one another again that each of you is willing to take that extra step to bring about reconciliation. Ask that each of you show compassion and understanding. And ask that they make it easy!

A birthmark is a kiss from an angel.

ANON

In earlier times it was believed that no-one should try to be perfect because to do so would be dishonouring God, the only one who is perfect. Therefore, artists who created such wonderful illuminated manuscripts as the Book of Kells would make a deliberate error in their work!

Therefore, what some people see as imperfection can, in reality, be something of exception. Today make sure you do not discard something simply because it's not absolutely perfect to your eyes; instead, imagine that that little imperfection is really a secret message saying an angel has had a hand in its design!

17 September

Look up into the September skies today at morning, noon and sunset. Watch as clouds form and reform, and the breeze moves them high up in the sky.

Let your imagination roam freely. Is that an angel that is moving across the sky, or is it merely a cloud? What messages do the emerging patterns give you? Are the angels trying to tell you something special?

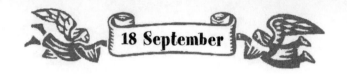

Call your angel any time – you'll never be put on hold.

SUZANNE SIEGEL ZENKEL, *YOUR SECRET ANGEL*

I'm often asked if there's a limit to the questions and requests you can ask of your angel. Is there a limit to the questions you can ask your parents, or your teachers? Of course not, so the simple answer is 'no'! You'll never be put on 'hold' but you may have to wait for 'Angel Time' before things become clear.

Why do we become afraid? Are we weak to admit fear? The answer is a definite 'no'! We become afraid when our ego forgets that it is connected with our spirit. Our spirit, which is the part always connected to God, or the Light Force, knows there is nothing to fear. It's the part of us that knows we are on a journey of enlightenment and that each step of the way brings us nearer to God. When we feel fear it's a message saying we are close, very close, to moving forward. If we felt no fear it would probably be a sign that we are static and there is no movement.

As Susan Jeffers's book, *Feel the Fear and Do It Anyway*, illustrates so well, we need to face that monster in front of us for it will never go away until we do. Of course, the truth is there is no monster, for fear is only a thought, not a reality. So, like a child, when you feel fear ask your angel to hold your hand as you take that next step. Take a deep breath in, step forward, and then breathe out.

I find it particularly helpful to imagine the situation after I've faced the fear. Let's say, for example, I had to face a court case and I was fearful of the outcome. Firstly, I'd ask that *'The Angel of Divine Love goes before me and prepares my way';* then I'd imagine that I was coming out of the court building, after the case had been heard, and I'd be feeling inside 'That was so much easier than I could ever have imagined.' By doing this I am not only putting my fear into a secondary position, I am also ensuring I will follow the course that will automatically bring about the outcome of 'That was much easier than I could ever have imagined.'

Do not wait for us. We are here.

ANGEL INSPIRATION

It's as though we've got the message upside-down. We don't have to become perfect in order to have our angels in our life. We don't have to wait around for our angels to contact us, they're already here; they've been with us since our spirit took its first flight into the Earth's atmosphere. We need now to understand that they're waiting for us to contact them! Just get on with it and don't waste any more time. Surrender to their knowing. Open up to their love. Do it now, accept their love into your life today.

Like angel visits – short and bright.

JOHN NORRIS, *MISCELLANIES*

Angels are 'beings of light' and therefore travel at the speed of light, which is very quick indeed! I find it easiest to see them when there is little or no interference from radio/televisual energies, or even electric lightbulbs! Today, watch TV by candlelight. Eat your supper with candlelight.

I see angels as little balls of light which dance around the room, or as larger-than-life human silhouettes in very bright golden light. If you want to see them, try not to stare at any 'vision' that you see. Instead, look with your 'third eye', which is your spiritual centre, based in the small dip between your eyebrows. So if you think you see an angel about, rather than stare unblinking at it, look just a little to the left or right of where the image has presented itself. It's really what's known as looking 'out of the corner of your eye' and it can require some practice.

Today is the day of the Autumn Equinox in the Northern Hemisphere (in the Southern Hemisphere it is on 22 March). From today the days will start getting noticeably shorter. Summer is over and the crops in the fields are almost all harvested. The seasons are changing once more.

Migratory birds such as swallows, are now ready to leave for warmer climes. Though the skies will seem emptier after their departure we know they will be back next summer. Before they leave, why not try the following ritual, which is based on an ancient Chinese custom. The birds act as the angels' messengers. If you have a problem that seems difficult to solve, take some cooked rice or breadcrumbs, and mentally put your requests into these small particles of food. Leave the food out for the birds and they will carry your messages up to God on behalf of you and your angels.

Today the Sun moves into the sign of Libra, seen as the 'scales of justice' or the 'bridge' between two warring parties. It is Archangel Uriel who looks after this sign, which has the element of Air. Like all Air signs, the characteristics of this solar month are to do with sorting out communication issues, and that can mean finding it easier to communicate with your angel, as well as the importance of feeling a sense of freedom, rather than feeling your life is becoming a prison-like structure.

Whether you're a Libran or not, the colours violet, white or indigo vibrate best with Archangel Uriel. Bring his energy into your world today by ensuring those colours are somewhere close to you. Wear a violet scarf or tie, carry a white handkerchief, purchase an indigo throw or cushion cover.

If you have any specific request for Archangel Uriel today, light a candle in violet, white or indigo, and ask for his special help.

Sometimes people ask me, 'Why isn't my life working when I've made so many changes?' The answer is because perhaps those changes aren't the right ones for you. If you have ever seen a young child trying to move from crawling to walking, you'll know that often the child will tumble before walking confidently. It takes time for that child to understand which is the best way to walk: the first time perhaps it's best to cling onto mummy's skirt, the next time there could be a table leg to hang onto. The third time the child finds it easiest to hold onto an adult's hands. Finally that child is walking without tumbling over! We're just the same. We all need to try out various methods and different patterns before we find the right one for us. Our angel is always there to point us in the right direction, but maybe we're not always listening! Don't be afraid to dump things that simply don't work. Congratulate yourself on making the first change, now make another! Keep saying, *'The Angel of Divine Guidance goes before me and prepares my way.'* Then, when you come up against any obstacles, you know you're just meant to face them and move on.

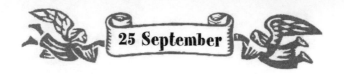

Whether you have your own garden or simply enjoy other people's 'green fingers', as the Sun moves lower in the sky, you cannot fail to see the changing season about you. Leaves change colour, flowers die back, and there can be a sense of sadness in our heart as we watch another year's growth come to an end.

Ask the Angel of Transformation to be with you at this time. She will help you understand that life is all about change and growth. The more aware you become of the cycles of the calendar year, the easier it becomes in your own life to welcome new cycles and let go of old ones. Remember it is not until we let go of something that's no longer good for us that we can offer a space in our life for something wonderful and new!

The michelmas daisy is associated with the month of September. Part of the aster family ('aster' means 'star'), they bloom at the end of September and are named after Archangel Michael whose feast day is 29 September.

Michelmas daisies have magnificent clusters of flowers which attract butterflies, and they add brightness to the autumn garden. If your angel garden has enough space, why not grow some michelmas daisies there next year? You need to sow seeds indoors from spring through summer, and they like well-drained soil. The seedlings should then be planted out by early summer for flowering at this time. You can, of course, buy seedlings in garden centres.

From now on, each time you see the cheerful, abundant michelmas daisy, remember it's named after Archangel Michael.

Do not whisper your name,
We know it well.

ANGEL INSPIRATION

There's no need to fear, your angel is with you right now and knows everything! There's no need to feel you're forgotten – your angel knows you and your needs.

When making important decisions, why not make a pact with your angel regarding 'the perfect outcome'? I always set up a particular scenario, and ask my angel to collaborate with me to synchronize the best solution. So, if I'm asked to give a workshop in a venue and I'm not sure if I should or not, I'll say to my angel *'Can you get ten people to book on it within the next three days if it's right for me to do this?'* Then if this happens, I know it's right. If less than ten book within the stated time, I realize that there's something else for me to do. Try a similar 'pact' with your angel today.

Calcite, which is a transparent or milky-pearl crystal, can help to bring about balance between the male and female polarities or the 'intuitive' and 'proactive' energies within each of us.

Take a 15-minute break away from demands and distractions. Find a comfortable place to sit or lie. Hold a calcite crystal in your left hand and place it across your heart. Close your eyes. Now ask Archangel Uriel to work with this crystal in order to help you harmonize your energies into perfect balance. Imagine the energy of the crystal moving from your left hand into your heart. From there it moves into your bloodstream and travels all the way around your body, from your head down to your feet. Gently open your eyes and return to the room, feeling much more balanced than before.

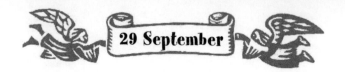

Today is the Feast of the Archangels. Light a candle to celebrate this day and place it on your indoor Angel Shrine. And what about filling a vase with flowers here, too? Imagine that you're celebrating a feast day for your greatest friends. What would you do? How would you honour your friends? Treat your archangels in the same way with a special celebration of your own making!

Meditate today.

It's the last day of September, and time to thank Archangel Uriel for being with us throughout the month. Light a white, indigo or silver candle in gratitude.

Take some time to yourself where you can spend a few minutes meditating. Breathe in deeply and let that breath out slowly. Do this until your breathing is steady and deep. Now go over the month in your mind. What are the high points? And the low points? Did you realize that Archangel Uriel was there to help you? Now thank this Archangel for all his help as you move forward into the next month.

The Angel of October

Barbiel

(Southern Hemisphere - Barbiel is the Angel of April)

It's harvest time at last! Now look back over the months and see just how far you have come! Barbiel, the Angel of October, reminds us of the generosity of nature, and at this time helps us understand 'as you reap, so shall you sow'. Some things we shall enjoy immediately, others we can keep until the optimum time.

Why not celebrate the fruits of the season by inviting Barbiel to join you at your table today, and remember to say 'thank you' for the abundance you share. Make special preparations for your main meal today. Choose fruits and vegetables of the season. Lay the table as if for an honoured guest, which Angel Barbiel certainly is! Have angel lights and candles, and you may even find some paper napkins with angel designs. Enjoy every moment of your special meal!

2 October

Today is the Druidic Feast of the Guardian Spirits.

The Druids knew that they were guided at all times by their 'anam cara' or 'soul friend'. They could call on their soul friend in times of need and would be able to share their courage and knowledge. Yet, like us, they realized that their 'anam cara' could only give advice and support, they still had to face the lesson themselves in order to gain enlightenment.

Burn a frankincense stick today, and as you breathe in the essence it will help you to attain a higher level of understanding of our connection with the spirit world from where we can gain so much knowledge. Be extra aware of the power of your dream messages tonight.

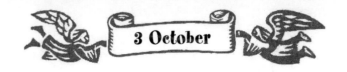

This is the time to plant the herb angelica, known as 'the food of the angels'. This deciduous shrub should be planted in the place where you wish it to grow, as moving it later can disturb its growth. It needs a certain amount of shade in order to flourish, and does well at the back of a border. Note that angelica can grow as high as 2 m/6½ ft and spread to almost the same width, so only plant it if you have plenty of space in your garden! Next summer you will be able to take its stems and cook them with rhubarb in order to sweeten it. You can also make a tea out of its leaves (see page 256), and use it for decorating desserts and cakes.

If you can't grow angelica, at least buy some candied angelica and add to your baking or desserts!

October's crystal is the opal, part of the quartz group of crystals. As opals need to be kept in humid conditions they are very much connected with the Moon and intuition.

If you cannot get hold of an opal, try to find a moonstone crystal. Do the following visualization out of doors, if you can, under the light of the Moon; otherwise stay indoors with the curtains open:

Hold the crystal in your left hand against your heart. Close your eyes and breathe in the power of the Moon. Try to connect with it, and the crystal should help you do this.

Know that your angels and spirit guides are trying to encourage you to be more intuitive and open to their guidance. If you find it difficult to accept guidance in this situation, ask that the angels share it with you while you sleep, in your dreams. Prepare to write down any dream messages on awakening.

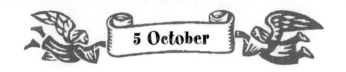

Tomorrow is World Angel Day. Get ready for this very special day by inviting friends or just one friend to come and share the celebration with you tomorrow. Prepare to cook something special for World Angel Day; it can be as simple as a pasta dish such as Angel Hair with Balsamic Tomatoes (see page 83), sprinkled with Parmesan cheese and black pepper. Clear away anything you've been hoarding and not using, and get your home ready for a party. Even if it's just for you and your angel, it's important to prepare your surroundings and honour your special guest.

You can make a simple candle ceremony by massaging sweet-smelling essential oils such as ylang-ylang, jasmine or rose into candles, and perhaps arrange a bowl of water with floating candles. As you organize yourself for tomorrow, think back on how your angel's presence has changed your life.

Praised be all the angels for ever.
TOBIT 11:15, THE BIBLE

Today is World Angel Day. Invite your angels and friends to a party! Perhaps even ask that each guest brings a special wrapped angel gift along the lines of a 'Kris Kringle', but put a ceiling on the price so that no-one need feel under any obligation to overspend.

Have an overall plan for the celebration, but allow room for spontaneity, as this is what the angels love most of all. What about beginning the celebration with a short meditation, lighting the sweet-smelling candles you prepared yesterday? Keep it simple, inviting each guest to meet their angel in a familiar place and show love and thanks for their presence in their lives. This can be followed by food, and then the sharing of gifts, where all the gifts are collected together and each guest chooses one. You can then share with each other how the angels have helped to change your lives. The more we all talk about our angels, the more angels can talk to us!

Cosmos are the flowers for the month of October. Cosmos have shocking pink flowers with yellow centres. The stems are very thin and are blown over easily by a strong wind. However, this seems more like a protective reaction to the buffeting of the wind for soon the cosmos rises again and looks up to the Sun with vigour.

These flowers can often symbolize our own 'rise and fall'. We, too, can be buffeted by the harsh winds of change. By ducking its main force we can rise again and stand tall and strong. To bend to the wind is often the best answer. Remember, the angels know our true course in life, but it's often our own stubbornness which destroys our growth. Instead of doggedly forcing issues, we may need to take time out and rethink our pathway. This apparent 'fall' can prove to be the best response to difficult times. Remember to ask your angel to give you simple guidance so that you know when to duck and when to stand tall!

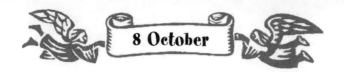

8 October

It's time to do some serious clearing out. This is the harvest time of the year now and no-one wants to harvest garbage!

It's not always easy to let go, though, so ask your angel to help you make some simple, straightforward decisions about what should go and what should stay. Go through your wardrobe today and see what you will wear and what is just hanging up, taking up space. Do you really need these things or are they just filling a void? If it's the latter, pack them up and ship them off to a needy person or a charity shop.

Today take some time out in the open air among trees and nature, for it is the magical workings of Mother Nature which cleanses the toxins in the air and gives us clean oxygen to breathe. Stand up against a tree. Lean your back into it. Now focus on the roots of that tree beneath your feet. Imagine that those roots are also connected with your feet. Feel the strength and stability of this tree. Breathe it into your body. Breathe in that strength. Breathe in the tree's certainty, that knowledge that despite rain, snow and harsh winter winds, its buds will push forth new life once springtime comes. Breathe in its flexibility. Feel the wind and winter gales try to force the tree to bend and succumb. Yet it doesn't. Its flexibility allows it to survive and thrive into the next year and new growth. Can you see how the tree and your own life can seem similar? Ask your angels to help you to be certain yet flexible as you move through your own seasons.

Have an 'Angel Day' today. It's simple, and it's fun. Get as many people involved in this as you can and you'll soon find your day is lightened and brightened! The word 'angel' comes from the Greek *angelos* which means 'messenger from God', and it holds within its sound great power. When you say this special word you are drawing towards you great impetus for positive energy everywhere you go.

All you need do is put the word 'angel' before any word of your choosing. For instance, have an 'angel breakfast' before leaving your 'angel home'. Give your loved ones an 'angel kiss' as you leave each other, and wish each other an 'angel day'. Enjoy your day with your 'angel colleagues' or 'angel friends', and have a satisfying 'angel lunch' ... Use your imagination and you'll soon be laughing as you add this special word to your sentences. Children can get into the swing of this very easily, so let them teach you how easy it is to have a wonderful 'Angel Day'! You might even decide to make every day an Angel Day!

If you have a garden, what about planting some angel fishing rods (*Dierama pulcherrimum*) for next summer? These are slender, arching stalks topped with pendulous, bell-shaped flowers of white, pink or magenta, hanging gracefully, looking just like fishing rods! Use along the edge of water or against a background of dark green shrubs. Bear in mind these evergreen perennials need full to partial sun. They are a fast-growing grass-like foliage which can reach up to 60 cm/2 ft, with flower stalks from 1–2 m/3–6 ft.

Angels are hardly strangers.

PENNY MARSHALL'S *THE PREACHER'S WIFE*

It's only in recent years that we've tended to lose sight of our angels. The good news is, they haven't lost sight of us! They aren't strangers, they are our greatest, closest friends. Talk to them now!

Sing an angel song today. You don't have to sing like an angel to sing an angel song! There is a myriad of lyrics to choose from: 'I'm Loving Angels Instead', 'I Believe in Angels', 'In the Arms of an Angel' ... Think of all the songs that mention the word 'angel'. Sing in the bath, under the shower, in the car, in the middle of a field ... sing wherever you feel like singing and, preferably, get others to join in with you.

14 October

Make an angel tablemat for 'an angel at my table'. Get some quality cardboard and cut it into the shape of a tablemat. Now draw and colour some pretty pictures. Use your imagination or, if you really feel stuck, cut out pictures from some source material and stick them onto the tablemat.

Each time you see this angel tablemat it will remind you that you are never alone as you sit at your table.

15 October

Be aware today. Take extra care to stop every hour on the hour of wakefulness and be aware. Listen. Look. Feel. Touch. Smell. Put a halt to the hurly-burly of everyday living and be aware. In that way you will be more aware of your angel's presence. It just takes some practice!

It's bulb-planting time! Plan ahead for next spring now. Plant some Angel Tears, otherwise known as *Narcissus triandus*, in your garden or, if you don't have a garden, plant some in pots for indoor flowering. They will give you a bright burst of colour in the spring and show themselves off particularly well against the brown leaves of a beech or the red of dogwood (*Cornus*). Angel Tears have small white and yellow flowers, and bear several to a stem. Bear in mind they need partial shade, and if you have your own Earth Shrine, this is the perfect place for them. (Should you be short on space, place the bulbs in a container which can be easily lifted out of the ground once the flowers have died down.) Ensure the bulbs are planted 8–10 cm/3–4 inches below the earth. If planting indoors, water and keep in a cool, dark space until the green shoots are about 5 cm/2 inches high. Then bring them out into a warmer environment where the sunlight can encourage them to thrive.

Do not search for us, we have already found you.

ANGEL INSPIRATION

Remember, no matter how bleak and lonely you may feel, your angels are here for you now. Do not look outwards for them, instead look inside yourself. Reach out to them, allow their gentle, strong wings to enfold you and keep you safe and secure.

The following is a simple yet effective visualization exercise which will help you to heal your inner child, that part of us which faced a difficult time in our early years when we were incapable of understanding what was happening and why.

Make sure you do this exercise when you are alone, without distractions. (If you like, record the following script, taking about 5–10 minutes to read it out loud.) Light a candle, play gentle music in the background and sit in a comfortable place.

Now imagine that you are in a garden or the countryside and you are watching the following scenario going on (as though it's a programme on TV). You see an angel is walking down the garden path. There are trees and bushes around the pathway but the angel seems to know exactly the direction to take. As you watch, you notice it's nearing sunset, and perhaps you can even see the bright Sun setting and feel its warm, gentle rays on your skin. You feel relaxed and calm as the scene unfolds.

Now you hear a child crying. As the angel continues along the path, the cries become louder. They are heart-wrenching sobs, and you realize the angel wants to find this child and console it. You see the angel walk off the path, following the cries. Now the angel finds the child and picks it up into its arms. As the child continues to cry, the angel calmly offers love and consolation. 'What can I do to help?' the child is asked. 'Why are you so upset?'

Suddenly you realize that this little child is you, yourself. Know that you are safe and secure, and the one being in your life who never judges you is here right now. Perhaps amid sobs or with just a gentle understanding you now discover what the problem has been. The angel gently enfolds you in its love amid assurances that it is here to love and guard you forever.

Why not contact some friends and like-minded people and develop your own 'Healing with Angels' group? You don't need to have a degree or diploma to start one, just an open mind and a willingness to share your knowledge and experiences with others. Nor do you need to know hundreds of people, or even have much space to welcome a group each week. Mention the possibility to one or two friends. Ask them to invite someone else. Immediately you have a small group of people interested! You can meet at any time that's convenient for you. All you need is a quiet room, perhaps some music playing, and some candles and incense sticks (frankincense is particularly helpful to heighten awareness).

Keep your meetings simple: a short visualization (see daily entries for 7 March, 22 March, 3 April, 28 September and 9 October for ideas), a chat about your experiences to date, any issues that are in your life right now ... Sharing and caring is all that's required to form firm friendships with others and your angels.

Today is the Chinese Festival of Ancestors. No matter what your culture, why not acknowledge those who have gone before us, those people on whose shoulders we often stand?

Think back over your life. Who has had an important influence on you? You are part of your heritage, part of your culture, part of your family tree. Yet you are unique, as well. Each generation needs to heal the last. With the help of our angels we can achieve this without too much disruption.

Sit quietly and contemplate the effect your family has had on you. Your own parents are products of their childhood, which must be remembered! Now ask your angel to be with you as you write a letter to each of your ancestors who has influenced you, even if you didn't ever meet them. Sometimes what you write might be angry, sometimes you may be surprisingly forgiving. Imagine those people are going to read your letter and take note of your words. Be honest, be truthful and try to end it with forgiveness.

21 October

Every day is a new chance to begin again. Say aloud, *'This is the first day of the rest of my life.'* Think about those words. They're true! You have a wonderful opportunity to change just one of your imbedded ideas today. Change your perception of life and life will change for you. Be impulsive. Do something without planning it in advance. Angels love an adventure, don't you?

Even though the days are beginning to be noticeably shorter we need to be planning ahead for the coming spring. This is a perfect time to plant roses and, even if you only have a patio space, what about seeing if you can find a thornless hybrid rose called 'Smooth Angel'? If your local garden centre cannot supply it, check out horticultural sites on the internet. Smooth Angel has large cream petals with warm apricot-yellow centres, and a very strong, sweet fragrance. Flowering from spring through summer, it grows quickly to a bushy form approximately 1.2 m/4 ft tall and is disease-resistant, an added bonus! (Prune it in late-winter to ensure vigorous growth next year.)

23 October

Today the Sun moves into the zodiac sign of Scorpio. Archangel Gabriel looks after this Water sign, so surround yourself with the colours blue, white and silver over the coming month to enhance this archangel's presence in your life.

As already stated, Archangel Gabriel looks after the artistic area of our lives, so get creative! The nights are drawing in, and the days are getting shorter. Use this period now to connect with spiritual guidance. Ask Archangel Gabriel to help you source your creativity. You don't need to spend much money to develop your creative skills – all you need is a pen or pencil and some paper! Start by drawing simple flowers or angels, birds and butterflies. Use colouring pencils or crayons to bring them to life with colour. The more you connect with your right brain, which is about creative expression and spirituality, the more easily you will connect with your angels.

Today is Archangel Raphael's feast day. Celebrate Raphael's influence in your life in the area of healing, whether it's in your own personal life or in healing the global problems of disease and addiction to negative behaviour patterns. Wear red today and light a red candle to honour Raphael in your indoor Angel Shrine. Write out a list of all the areas in your life which Raphael has influenced, then write a letter of appreciation to him.

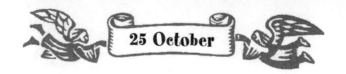

*Trust comes from within. The only one you
need to trust is yourself.*

ANGEL INSPIRATION

When I began giving my angel workshops I often wondered if
I was qualified to act as facilitator to those who came. Yet I
always seemed to find answers to their questions, and what I
said sounded credible! I received the above message myself in
the early years when I wasn't quite sure if I was doing the
right thing.

Sometimes it may seem easier to put our trust in others.
Perhaps they are better educated so we feel they must know
the answer. Not necessarily! Often we can feel betrayed by
the outcome, yet the only person who can betray us is ourself.
For when we trust our 'inner self' (which is our intuition connected with 'the Universal Mind', the Source or God) we can
never be betrayed. But if we bypass this and, instead, put
more trust in what someone else says, we are risking the
possibility of going down the wrong road.

26 October

Take a walk in a place of nature today. Watch as the leaves fall from the trees. The trees are getting ready to sleep for winter. Thank them for the shelter, beauty and life-giving gifts they have given us during the year.

27 October

At this time of the year, the Hindu population will be celebrating Laksmi, otherwise known as the Festival of Light. Laksmi is the Hindu goddess of prosperity and, if we wish her to visit our home, we must make sure it is spick and span! It is known that 'nature abhors a vacuum', so the more old stuff that is flung out, the more likelihood that good things will take its place. During this festival at dusk, lamps and candles are lit in every room and outside, too. The windows are then opened and Laksmi is invited into the home to bless the house and its occupants.

You don't have to be of this culture to celebrate something similar. Clean up your home, light candles in each room and invite the Angels of Divine Abundance to come into your home and stay there for as long as you wish. Make sure to celebrate the new beginning of abundance in your life with some sort of food and drink.

Say 'thank you' today. Check out your Earth Shrine and see if it needs any new object added to it, or if it needs a general tidy up.

We don't have to say 'thanks' to Mother Nature or our angels, but showing gratitude is showing a 'great attitude'. When we have enough, it brings us more. When we say 'thanks' for the lessons we need to learn it helps us accept change and challenge. It helps us understand and move free from the clouds of uncertainty towards clarity.

All around the circle of the sky
I hear the Spirit's voice.

NATIVE AMERICAN SAYING

It is no accident that all the ancient cultures speak of a higher source, a spiritual connection between mankind and God. Believing in the spirit world and angels is no 'New Age' fad, it's many thousands of years old. Such ancient traditions deserve to be recognized for what they are, based in deep-seated knowledge and understanding of the truth about life on Earth. By opening up our understanding of the origin of symbolism, myths and legends, we can empower ourselves and each other.

Today seek out more information about other cultures. Go to a bookshop or a library and look for publications on ancient cultures and religions. If you have an internet connection, go into a search engine and seek information on these areas for yourself. You'll be amazed at what you find!

Are you having difficulties with anyone in particular? Perhaps the person causing most trouble is really a 'blessing in disguise'! Think about this for a moment, though it might seem difficult to believe, it is a possibility. Are you being forced out of your 'comfort zone', which is a safe but limiting situation, by this person? What changes can you make in your life because of the difficulties you perceive?

Do this short but effective ritual to begin to heal what you see is the problem:

Get approximately 60 cm/2 ft of ribbon (gold, white, pink or blue) and tie the ends together, then lay it out in a figure of 8. Place a slip of paper with your name on it in one of the circles, and the name of the other person in the other circle. Place a candle (in pink or blue) on top of the names, and where the two circles entwine, place a symbol of an angel. Light the candles. Close your eyes and ask the Angel of Divine Healing to come into the situation now. Ask the Angel to help you to understand what you need to know. Sit quietly for a few minutes. Think back over your relationship with this person. What are you learning from each other? When you feel ready, say aloud that person's name and then *'The Light within me salutes the Light within you.'* Imagine that the Angel of Divine Healing is now gently separating the circles and you are now both free of the problems between you. As each of you learn the necessary lessons you no longer need to face difficulties together. Thank the Angel of Divine Healing for being here today and open your eyes. Let the candles burn out if possible.

This morning thank Barbiel, the Angel of October, for all the abundance you have enjoyed this month, and also for showing you that what you have sown you have reaped in the long-term.

In the Northern Hemisphere, today is the Celtic Festival of Samhain, which marks the first day of the Celtic New Year. (In the Southern Hemisphere, Samhain is celebrated on 1 May.) The Angel of the South is here with you today, encouraging you to open up to daily spiritual connection, trying to help you understand the meaning of the seasons of our lives. 'Samhain' means burning the bones, when our ancestors brought the bones of those elders who had died during the past 12 months together in order to honour their lives in a mass ceremony. (It is from this 'bone fire' where we get the word 'bonfire'.)

This season is all about silence, darkness, connectedness. The quieter your life, the more likely you can connect with angels and spirit beings. Now, with the long winter months ahead, there is no time like the present to focus on your own spiritual development.

The following is a short visualization exercise you can enjoy tonight as the Sun sets below the horizon. As always when meditating, make sure you will not be disturbed and sit in a comfortable position. You may like to record the exercise for yourself and play it back at your leisure. (It should be of 10–12 minutes duration.)

Sit quietly and close your eyes. Breathe deeply and let any cares or concerns go to the back of your mind. Now imagine you are walking in the dark. It's a long, lonely road which offers no light at all. Moving along it is quite a struggle, for you don't know where you are and you cannot see where you are going. Perhaps you sense trees close by but their presence doesn't give you much comfort. Fortunately, you now realize your angel has just made itself known to you. Its brightness lights the way for you. Now you come to a crossroads. Your angel takes your hand and leads you forward. Any darkness is now dissipated and you see the trees about you are lit up by the devas dancing among their branches. What was once threatening is now inviting. You know you have now taken the right road and your angel is leading you forward effort-lessly. You feel a weight of anxiety lift from you as you move forward.

In the distance, on the horizon, the new dawn is beginning to shed its light. Your heart is open to this light as you breathe in deeply, filling your lungs and diaphragm, and then breath-ing out, once more you are aware of your feet and your hands. Again, breathing in deeply and then breathing out, you feel your entire body from your head all the way down to your toes. Then breathing in deeply again and breathing out, you are now ready to open your eyes and return to this room. You feel relaxed and optimistic for the new year ahead.

The Angel of November

Adnachiel

(Southern Hemisphere - Adnachiel is the Angel of May)

1 November

The nights are longer and very little is growing outside. It is with Adnachiel, the Angel of November, that we can enjoy the harvest we have collected from our hard work earlier in the year. Adnachiel urges us to show thanks to others who have supported us throughout the year, not least the beings of the devic kingdom. November is also a good time to clear away all the dead growth in the garden (and we can do that symbolically in our own life too!). As you clear away the old growth, remember to collect seeds for sowing next year. You are then being a minister to the cycles of life, developing within you a deeper understanding of the need for death before we can be reborn to grow again.

The word 'occult' can sometimes have fearful connotations, yet it is the word for light that is cut off at regular intervals, such as the light of a lighthouse. It is there, but it is not seen. We all have innate abilities to tune into what is there but not seen, the spiritual world. Today burn a purple candle to honour Adnachiel's presence in your life this month and, if necessary, ask for extra help to connect with your inner powers.

2 November

Spiritus, the divine breath, inspiration.
And now it's your turn to give it back.
That's how the whole thing works.

STEPHEN SPIELBERG'S *ALWAYS*

We come into the world taking a deep breath in and breathing out, and we leave the world in the same way. Yet, as adults, very few of us breathe correctly. Though we're born with the ability to breathe deeply into our diaphragm we tend to take shortcuts and breathe only into the upper part of our lungs. Apart from causing stress, this habit is not conducive to spiritual connection. If you practise yoga or deep meditation you will already know the importance of deep breathing.

From today take at least three deep breaths when you awaken and again as you go to sleep. Breathe deeply into the centre. When you form this healthy habit you will find you are not only detoxifying your body with each outward breath, you are also firmly in touch with your integral self, and with spirit.

The crystal for November is topaz, a Sanskrit word meaning 'Fire' or 'Heat'. Mostly a golden yellow in colour, the topaz can help to lighten our load emotionally, and enlighten us creatively. Topaz is also good for detoxifying the body and improves the thyroid and metabolism.

Try to surround yourself with yellow this month. Buy a reasonably priced yellow throw, cushion covers, mugs and plates. Wear a yellow scarf or a handkerchief. Yellow is the symbol of the Sun and we all need that colour around us as the days turn darker and the nights draw in.

In a time of quiet, ask your angel to be with you. Massage a yellow candle with lemon or citronella essential oil (starting at the centre of the candle, and moving down it to Earth and up it to Heaven), and when the candle is lit, close your eyes and take a deep breath, filling up both lungs as you breathe in and out. Now imagine that flame of light is within you. It's at the very integral part of you, your spiritual centre, flickering sometimes, at other times burning proud and bright. Imagine that flame is now growing bigger and brighter inside you. It's lighting you up from within, enlightening you with wisdom and joy. All the while you imagine it's growing bigger, it's filling your body from your centre down to your legs and toes, up to your chest, head and arms. When you feel completely filled with the light, ask your angel if you need to know anything right now. Listen and feel the answer. Then thank your angel for being with you and now open your eyes to a brighter, lighter world!

I believe we are free, within limits, and yet there is an unseen hand, a guiding angel, that somehow, like a submerged propeller, drives us on.

RABINDRANATH TAGORE

If you are angry with your angels at any time for apparently not being with you when you needed them, think again. As already stated, we each have free will and our angels cannot force us against that will. Angels guide us gently, but do not shove! Be aware of that, and be honest with yourself should you be going through rough times. Are you listening to what you should be doing, or are you merely stubbornly refusing to hear? Don't blame the angels, don't blame yourself. Just make the necessary changes.

In the Northern Hemisphere, the Celtic Festival of Samhain continues throughout the months of long, dark nights and short days. Very little work can be done out of doors at this time, except for clearing things up from the last harvest. Instead, it's the part of the year where people stay indoors and contact the spirit world. There are many forms of 'divination', which means getting in touch with the Divine (God). Flames, whether from rush lights, candles or fires, have always held fascination, and ancient peoples all over the globe have used them in order to divine the future.

You can practise the following ritual alone or with others. If the latter, have each person take a turn at 'reading' the flames of the candles. (This method is known as 'lychnomancy'.) Place three white candles in a triangle-shape. If possible, leave an emblem of an angel in the middle (a picture, figure, even your angel's name written on a piece of paper). Light the three candles and wait for a few moments for them to burn steadily. Turn off the lights so that you are now working in candlelight only. Now ask your angel to give you guidance through the flames of these candles on various issues of your life. Ask for help on each issue separately. Close your eyes, take a deep breath, breathe out and open your eyes. Watch how the flames are burning.

Sputtering: take matters into your own hands and make definite choices.

Wavering unsteadily: suggests uncertainty and/or that you could be involved in several different things.

Rising high then decreasing: you need to fully commit yourself and focus on the long-term.

Rising high and burning steadily: keep to your path, success is on the way.

One or more candles are extinguished: stop the course you are on and take another direction.

Close your eyes again and ask your angel to give you more guidance, if required. Douse the flames and re-light the candles for the next question.

Chrysanthemum is the flower for November. They come in a variety of sizes and colours, and brighten up the dull early winter days. If you have been given a pot of chrysanthemums and want to plant them for next year, cut them down to 23 cm/9 inches from the ground and remove all the leaves. Dig them up and gently lifting them from the ground, plant in seed trays filled with moist topsoil, potting compost or peat. Place them in a cool but frost-free place over the winter months. In the spring, take cuttings and plant in your angel garden. They will flower once more in the following October/November.

Chrysanthemums have always been known as the flowers of protection and healing. A warm drink can be made from a mixture of 5 g/¼ oz of peppermint leaves and 5 g/¼ oz of chrysanthemum leaves. Put the leaves in a warmed teapot or cup, pour boiling water over them and leave for 10 minutes or so before drinking. This can help allay the misery of colds.

Fear: we can't buy it but we can certainly buy into it! Fear seems like our greatest enemy, yet it can be our greatest strength, once we face it. If we refuse to face it, it may grow out of all proportion, and we can believe we are being overwhelmed by it.

Sit quietly and focus on what fears lie hidden in your heart. Focus on just one fear. Choose a word for it, such as 'poverty' if you fear having no money, or 'loneliness' if you feel you can't find a partner. Now think of the opposite word to that which you have chosen, i.e. 'wealth' instead of 'poverty', or 'love' instead of 'loneliness'. Keep saying that word to yourself, say it aloud, sing it, dance to it, write it on sticky labels and leave them around your house and your car. Soon you will find these positive situations are now yours.

Today it is the festival of the Hearth. The hearth is the traditional place in the home for cooking and nourishing.

Don't just cook and eat today, make sure you savour every moment of its preparation and ingestion. Clean your cooker or microwave and be aware of the health and nutrition you gain from this area of your home. Cook some of your favourite food today and be very aware of its taste and goodness as you enjoy it. Leave a little of your food on a small plate in your kitchen for the angels of the hearth and later give it to the birds who will carry it away to Heaven with their blessings.

9 November

There's no time like the present to prepare for the festive season coming up. Remember those Salt Dough Angels that you made at the beginning of August? Well, now is the time to make some more (see page 247 for directions). These Dough Angels make perfect Christmas decorations, and also lovely personalized gifts for your friends. If you're making them as Christmas gifts, why not write special messages such as 'Mary's Angel' or 'My Kitchen Angel' in the dough, using a sharp knife? Use your imagination!

Incubate a dream tonight. Make sure your bed and bedroom is comfortable and airy. Put a couple of drops of lavender essential oil on either side of your pillow, and if you have an amethyst crystal, keep that close to your bed as it will help you connect more easily with your angel as you sleep.

As you are getting comfortable, go through the issues on your mind and think of just one. Now ask your angel to help you get the correct guidance to help you sort out this problem through a dream. Ask that the dream be as simple and uncomplicated as possible. If you want to know whether you should go in one particular way, ask your angel to make it very obvious if you are correct in doing so. Tell yourself that when you awaken you will easily remember parts of the dream, especially how you felt. Were you happy in the dream or were you terrified? If on waking you discover you felt happy, then your angel is telling you to go ahead with your plans; if the opposite, make new plans!

11 November

This is the time to remember those who have passed on, especially in conflicts all over the world. Remember that peace is not gained through conflict with others, peace must begin within our own hearts. It is based on acceptance, compassion and the knowledge that each and every one has an angel and is loved by that angel. When we accept this we shall no longer live in fear, nor have it reflected outside ourselves in conflict.

Take a pink or red candle and massage it with jasmine or ylang ylang essential oil (starting at the centre of the candle and then moving down it to Earth and up it to Heaven). If you have a rose quartz crystal, place this near the candle and light it. Focus on the candle flame and close your eyes. Feel peace develop within your heart based on the foundation of angelic love that you know is within you. Now ask that the Angel of Divine Peace goes before you in all that you do every day of every year. Ask that the Angel of Divine Peace goes before all world leaders every hour of every day of every year so that they will make the choices which are right for peace and goodwill.

12 November

The windows of the world are covered in rain
Whenever rain appears it's really angel tears
How long must they cry?
BURT BACHARACH, *THE WINDOWS OF THE WORLD*

Have you ever wondered if our life on the Planet Earth is just an experiment? When I hear the news sometimes I feel strongly that the experiment went very wrong, but then my belief will be reborn again with a random act of kindness, an unexpected gift, a supportive phone call ... What do the angels think of us? Why can we not get on?

Today imagine that you can see the angels walking beside everyone you meet. Yes, even those who push into you and are generally mean-minded, they too have an angel (though they're obviously not listening to them!). Take this idea into your workplace, into your home, onto the road way as you travel by foot or by vehicle. See how your perception of people, and of life, changes when you recognize that everyone has an angel!

If the stores are open in your area today, visit a bookshop and search the shelves for books on angels. Alternatively, go to the local library, or if you're housebound use the internet. See the multitude of words which have been written about these 'beings of light'. As you read the poetry or prose, just for a few moments connect yourself with all those other millions of people who are doing the same all over the world. Try to imagine a tiny golden strand of light connecting you all.

Death is not a punishment. Death is a gift because that spirit has decided to move on from the lessons of the Earth and enjoy further growth and spiritual enlightenment. As the spirit guide Emmanuel states in *Emmanuel's Book* (compiled by Pat Rodegast and Judith Stanton), 'Death is like taking off a tight shoe ... Death is freedom of the physical.' Countless people have enjoyed proof of life after death from their loved ones, and from their own near-death experiences.

Celebrate the life of someone you loved who died in recent years. Talk about them, share their stories, laugh at your joint experiences. Don't hide from death. Cry, express your grief at your loss, and remember their spirit is still alive. If you need to forgive them, ask your angel to find it in your heart to do so. Once that person has left this world they are no longer tied to the old ways of thinking and their own fears. If you fear that they did not forgive you for something you may have done, release this fear now. Send each other love instead.

Listen to the quiet voice within ... Trust it for it is
your very essence and it will never play you false ...
And know this: once you have set your feet upon
the path that you know is the right one for you,
your whole life will light up!

FRANK SMITH, *CHILDREN OF LIGHT*

Whether from your angel or your spirit guide, the inner voice is coming from spirit. When you listen, then you will soon find your feet on the right path and things will begin to go right for you. It really can be as simple as that!

Get into the habit of taking 5 or 10 minutes just to yourself every day, preferably early in the morning when you are relaxed and fresh. Close your eyes and centre yourself. Now ask for guidance for the day ahead.

Imagine yourself going through the day without obstacles in your path. You know your angel is with you, guiding you gently.

16 November

Take out a video that involves an angel's presence: *Wings of Desire, Always, City of Angels, Michael, The Preacher's Wife,* to name just a few. Enjoy the fact that many, many people have been involved in making these movies, and many millions of viewers have been touched by the messages these stories have brought them. You're not alone in your belief in angels, it's just that we haven't all come 'out of the closet' about them as yet!

If you have children, watch the videos with them and encourage them to speak about their own angels.

Angels take note of everything we do.
(The angels have noted your good deeds.)

ANGEL INSPIRATION

How often have you done someone a good turn and got a (metaphorical) slap in the face for your efforts? Don't give up doing things to help others, but just don't expect to get thanks from the person you have helped. You will get repaid in other ways, though, and through other people. My mother used to tell me as a child when I did someone a good turn, 'The Recording Angel is recording', and I would have my generosity returned in some way. It works! So when you are on the receiving end of someone's 'random act of kindness' accept it with thanks, knowing it's just been passed on to you via 'the Recording Angel'!

18 November

Today is about trust. In the long, dark nights of winter it can be difficult to trust that there is light at the end of the tunnel! Although trust and hope are often paired, they are two different things. Hope is a passive act, filled with desire but static. Trust is active. When you trust that you are being guided with your angel's help along your pathway, you move forward step by step, sure that you are going the right way, knowing without question that you will be gently guided to take the right turn. Do you trust your angel?

The Angel of Release is with you today. What do you need to release in order to move onwards in your life experiences? Holding on to people, things or memories which were painful to us does not hold any benefit in the present. We need to release in order to leave space for new opportunities. The Angel of Release can help you to let go: let go of old ideas, let go of your children, let go of your loved ones who have passed on, let go of judgement of yourself and others.

Get some writing paper and write a letter to whoever has hurt you. Be as abusive as you wish! Write with a red pen (denoting anger and passion!) and imprint your words into the paper. Say how hurt you were, talk about how your life was affected by whatever happened. When you've done that, sign your name at the bottom with today's date, then light a white candle and burn the letter! Your angel will ensure that the anger and hurt are transmuted into light as the paper burns. Never, ever send such a letter to anyone. The reason for this ritual is to cleanse it once and for all from your emotions.

20 November

Today is the United Nations 'Rights of the Child' Day.

Take the time to really enjoy a child's company today. Become like a child again yourself and have fun, leaving your cares to tomorrow and creating joy and pleasure in this moment now! Go to a playground, invite some kids over, make something special together today.

What better time than to bring angels of love and protection into the children's world. Go through some magazines and find pictures of angels to cut out, and make a scrapbook of angels! Encourage the children to talk about their own angels, and explain how they are always with them, no matter what. Teach them to say *'The Angel of Divine Love and Protection goes before me today and every day!'* Make it into a song and sing the words together. The main message for today is, 'Be a child and enjoy a child's company in peace and in love.'

21 November

From the time you were conceived, my friend,
Until the time of death,
The angels, they are with you,
With each and every breath.

LEIGH ENGEL, *ANGELS ARE ALWAYS THERE*

Why don't angels show themselves to us more readily, especially when our lives seem to be going downhill? That's a question that I'm often asked at workshops. The answer I have is that it's up to us to reconnect with them. They cannot hit us over the head (though they may want to on occasion!). Their presence in our lives is a little like the internet: always available, but you have to turn it on and tune in order to get online!

Make a special effort today to make room in your life for your angel. Make extra space at the table, have a conversation with them in your mind. Incorporate the exercises and rituals in this book into your daily life. The more you do this, the easier it is to feel your angel's presence.

Today the Sun moves into the Fire sign of Sagittarius. Sagittarius is often seen as an archer, shooting an arrow forward and following where it is found. The best traits of Sagittarius, which is governed by the planet Jupiter, are friendliness, fun and generosity. The worst are impatience, lack of commitment and extravagance.

Archangel Raphael, who looks after this sign, can help us all, no matter our zodiac sign, to heal any negative traits and consequent feelings of failure. Sagittarius is also the sign of the sage (which is where it gets its name). By sharing joy, light and knowledge with all of us, we can be given the wisdom to expound on our belief in angels and their guidance to others, and so begin to energize love around the world.

Invite Archangel Raphael into your life today by lighting a yellow candle. Being the month of a Fire Sign, it's good to encourage warmth and energy into our lives by wearing warm russets, ochres and deep orange during this period.

Share your wings with those who have trouble flying.

ANON

Everyone on the Planet Earth is here to learn. When we learn one lesson we go on to the next, and often people that we taught a certain lesson to can now become our teachers for a different subject that we need to learn. It's a continuous experience of learning and teaching, teaching and learning. During our life's journey we can ask for help from other people, from our higher self and, of course, from our angels. Then we can pass on help to the person who is one step behind us. Just as the angels share their wings with us, we can share our wings with those who may have trouble flying. Do you know anyone right now who may need to share your wings?

24 November

Open your heart to the sound of silence and you shall
hear the wonders of all that exists.

ANGEL INSPIRATION

There is mystery in the sound of silence. Often we can be fearful of sitting in silence. Instead, we send a text message, chat to a friend, go onto the internet, turn on the TV... anything to distract us from sitting alone and getting to know ourself.

Today spend at least 15 minutes sitting quietly, with all the gadgets in your life turned off! Let your 'chattering mind' take a short break and breathe in deeply, deep into your diaphragm. Listen to your breathing and then as you get used to this allow some questions to surface in your mind. Soon you will find the answers come to you in the easiest of ways. Remember the answers, they're important!

If you're going shopping today, ask your angel to come along and make its presence known in some way. If you find it difficult to leave the house, it could be a message saying 'Don't go shopping today' and you should listen to this; no doubt there's something else you should be doing. However, if everything goes according to plan, you'll know your angel is paving the way for you on your shopping trip.

Should you have anything special that you need to find, tell your angel what it is before you leave the house. Then trust your instinct regarding precisely where you go to find it. Quite often it's the little things, such as finding a car parking space in an unusual spot, that will lead you to the precise shop where you can buy your promised purchase. If you find you're going from one shop to another, fruitlessly searching, then stop. That's a message saying today is not the day to find what you are looking for. Don't worry, there will be plenty more chances!

Check out Christmas cards with angels depicted on them. See how much the messages of the angels' presence in our lives is expanding worldwide. They are no longer restricted to ancient stories or children's tales, they are here now!

If you can't find any angel greeting cards, why not make some yourself? All you need is heavy paper or card, glue, glitter and pens/crayons/paints. Ask Archangel Raphael to help you bring light into the lives of the people to whom you are sending the cards. You'll soon find yourself inspired! Don't try to be perfect, just enjoy making the cards. The recipients will gain not only the gift of your artistry, but also the love and enthusiasm with which you made them.

It's nearly time to begin the season's decorations. While you're out shopping see how many angel-related decorations you can find. You might see shop windows with angels depicted in their decor, or buy some small angels for your Christmas tree. Treat it as a game with yourself or with children. When you get home, what about making a stencil of an angel? All you will need is a picture of an angel (use last year's Christmas cards, or see page 34 for templates of angels if you're stuck!) Go over the outline making a copy onto tracing paper and then transfer the outline onto more sturdy material such as heavy paper, cardboard or even a linocut. You can then use the stencil to decorate your windows, white paper napkins, greeting cards, table place-names, plain gift-wrap paper, kitchen presses, and so on. Make sure you use water-based paints so that they can be easily washed off afterwards, where necessary! (Buy some 'testers' in different colours; they don't cost much and are just right for painting the stencils.)

November is a great month for using your innate divinatory abilities to receive guidance. 'Ornithomancy' is simply observing birds in flight, how they feed and their song. The ancients believed that, as birds flew high up in the sky, they were in connection with God in the Heavens and therefore could bring messages of the future down onto the Earth. The great thing about this divinatory tool is you can practise it looking out through a window at work, in a vehicle or in your own home. You can, of course, stand outside, too, but it might be a bit cold at this time of the year!

Simply think of a question that you need answered. Close your eyes. Tell your angel what the question is. Now open your eyes and look up into the sky. How are the birds flying: in formation, singly, in couples, or are they diving through the sky with the wind? Are they making patterns that you can read? Are they almost out of sight? Are there no birds to be seen? Can you hear them singing? Is there just one bird in song or a cacophony of sound? How are they feeding? Are they fighting over a worm or a seed, or does each bird have its own meal? Consider the following divinatory responses:

Birds dipping and diving: don't be too serious, have a bit of fun and share your ideas.

Birds flying in formation: focus on one goal and one goal only.

Several birds in flight: work with others in order to achieve your goal.

No birds: time to take a rest and do nothing.

One bird in song: now is the time to state your case, you will be heard.

A cacophony of song: join with others, work together, bring about harmony.

Fighting over food: be careful of your income, there may be difficult times ahead.

Each eating separately: they'll be more than enough for everyone.

Feeding their young: nurture yourself.

As the days become shorter and the ground grows colder, make sure you are sharing your food with the wild birds of your neighbourhood. Feeding them with nuts and seeds will ensure they survive the long winter months and will bring new life, song and colour into your garden or environment throughout the coming year. Try to provide shelter for birds if possible. Just a nesting box hanging from a balcony, tree or bush left to its own devices without interference over the winter will give a home to these little beings which bring so much harmony and joy into everyone's life. Whatever you do for these little creatures with wings can be symbolic of looking after your own angels, too!

Thank the Angel of November, Adnachiel, for being with you throughout the short days and long nights of November. Adnachiel has helped you to open up your own divinatory abilities and, with this increased self-knowledge, you are more capable now of connecting with all the spiritual guidance which is available to you.

On this day, traditionally Thanksgiving Day, light lots of yellow candles to honour not only Adnachiel but also all the angels in your life who have helped you to find the right thing to do at the right time.

The Angel of December

Hanael

(Southern Hemisphere - Hanael is the Angel of June)

1 December

In the Northern Hemisphere, the nights are long, and the hours of the Sun are short and getting shorter. (June is the equivalent month in the Southern Hemisphere.) Winter is a time of deep sleep in the pastoral world around us. As growth dies down and lies beneath the surface of the soil, it reminds us that all physical life must come to an end but that our spirit always lives on.

Try to spend more time in the comfort of your home this month. Hanael, the Angel of December, will help us enjoy the balance of giving and receiving in many different ways: working and relaxing, giving our support to others and allowing ourselves to receive it in our own lives, the financial balance of income and expenditure, having fun with friends and having a quiet time alone to replenish our energy. Try not to overdo things this month, you simply won't have the energy because the days are quite literally too short!

2 December

A handmade gift says so much about the love and attention the maker has put into it. Make some **Marzipan Angels** today – this is so simple, and even a child can enjoy making them.

All you'll need is some marzipan, some candied peel and angelica, a little icing sugar ... and a sense of fun! A bar of cooking chocolate and natural food colorants are optional. Copy some pictures of angels or use the templates for angels on page 34 as the outline.

Sieve some icing sugar onto a clean surface so that the marzipan doesn't stick to it. Knead and roll out the marzipan until it's easy to handle. Then simply cut out the angel shapes you wish with a sharp knife. You can dip some in melted cooking chocolate. Use candied peel and angelica for the angel's eyes, nose and mouth. You can also add some colouring to a little of the marzipan to make hair, wings, halo, flowers, clothing. Use your imagination and have a lot of fun! Leave in a cool place to harden. Store in an airtight container.

3 December

No matter where you go, at this time of the year there are carols being sung in streets, shopping malls and over the radio and TV. See how many carols you know with 'angel' mentioned within its words: 'Angels we have heard on high...', 'The First Noel', 'Ding Dong Merrily ...' ...the list is endless! Make it into a competition with friends, family and children. Then, if you can't beat them, you may as well join them! Start singing some carols yourself, but only those with 'angels' mentioned. You might also like to form a singing group which could sing carols for charity in your neighbourhood.

4 December

Do you remember the Pasta Angels I suggested you make back in the summer? (See page 221 for details.) Well, now it's time to make some Pasta Angels for this festive season. Just follow the instructions as before, then hang the angels on your tree. Have fun!

Turquoise is the crystal for December. This beautiful blue stone has many properties in the healing area. It can be used for bringing calm into a situation, and it can revitalize the blood and bring about tissue regeneration in the body. It's also the colour of the thymus chakra, which is found between the heart and the throat chakra. The thymus is about unconditional love and the ability to speak up in a humanitarian manner in order to help those who are unable to help themselves.

Hold a turquoise crystal in your hand or wear it close to your throat. Imagine yourself in a situation of chaos where you can bring calm and serenity with your words. Imagine places on the planet where there is anger and fear. Ask your angel to travel with you to those places in your mind's eye. Now breathe unconditional love into those areas. Know that with your angel's help you can make a difference.

6 December

In the Christian church, today is traditionally the Feast of St. Nicholas, and he is the instigator of the man we now know as Santa Claus.

Today you and your angel can act as Santa Claus to someone in need. Look around your neighbourhood, there is surely someone who feels lonely, unloved and dreads this time of year. This year help make it different! Ask your angel what you can do to show a generous heart today. Your gift does not have to cost much, for no amount of money can bring happiness to someone who feels so low. What can bring happiness is the feeling that they are cared for by their angel. Look for a significant message, a little note, a tiny angel emblem. Make something yourself, or write a message in a card. If you can afford a small financial token this can be included. Send this gift with unconditional love to that person in the post or drop it through their letter box. Like Santa Claus, it is not necessary for you to meet in person.

7 December

Holly is the plant for the month of December.

We celebrate many ancient rituals during the darkest days of winter which have, in recent centuries, been adapted to more modern beliefs. Did you know that the reason we bring holly and ivy into the house at this time is to invite the devas into the warmth of our homes? That's been a tradition throughout Europe for thousands of years. It was to say, 'You've looked after all our pastoral needs over the spring, summer and autumn, now we want to look after you during the cold winter frosts.' By inviting the devas indoors we are ensuring that they will still be here to help us out during the next growing season!

Wherever you live, bring some holly into your home at this Yuletide. Try to resist holly with berries, though, as these are food for the birds. Instead, tie red ribbons in the holly for decoration and sprinkle some 'angel confetti' into it so that these glittering angel motifs will catch the light and sparkle back at you.

Hush! my dear, lie still and slumber,
Holy angels guard thy bed!
Heavenly blessings without number
Gently falling on thy head.

ISAAC WATTS

As you lie in bed tonight say the above words out loud to yourself. Then think about the words. They are full of gentleness and love. Share them with someone else, too.

There's nothing so precious as a handmade gift. Today make your own special Angel Inspiration cards for someone you love. Ask your angel to be with you as you do this; it's much easier than you may think!

All you'll need is some card, possibly in different colours, which you cut up to make cards approximately 9 x 4 cm/3 x 1½ inches. You can use a selection of different coloured felt-tip pens/pencils/crayons, some glitter, and any other decoration you like. Now, think of the person who will be receiving this gift. Think deeply about them. What motivates them? Why do you care for them? Remember your own angel knows too, and can give you the inspiration you need to make this the best gift ever!

Use the inspirational messages in this or other books, or make up your own.

Choose the messages you like and weave a love spell into your cards.

Look around your neighbourhood today. Who needs help and how can *you* help? No matter how financially strapped we may feel, there is always someone out there who is worse off. Are there organized charities already set up that you could give something to, or would you prefer to make up a 'Christmas Box' of your own? If you want to do this, keep it simple: staple foods mixed with a couple of little luxuries. You don't have to give in money terms, there are other options: what about visiting someone in hospital? Collecting for a charity? Bringing a less able-bodied person shopping? Think back on how much help and support you've received over the year and commit to passing on the gift now. If you're stuck for choices, ask your angel to point you in the right direction! Once you're open to helping out, you can be sure your angel will know where to send you!

This year, why not make your own Christmas cards? If you have access to a computer, you can use the designs available and simply print them out, making up your own greetings as you go. It's more fun, however, if you actually make your own from scratch. The simplest design, the shortest message is all that's required.

What does this season mean to you? What special message would you like to send your loved ones? Perhaps you could make up your own pictures of angels, or else use the angel templates on page 34. If you still have the cards you received last year, you could cut out some illustrations, or copy them in your own hand. Handmade, personalized messages mean such a lot to the receiver, especially when you make up a special verse for each person. Go on, have a go, you don't have to be perfect, just show how much you care!

12 December

What is most essential today
Is honesty, truth and love.
Truth and love cannot be separated,
They walk hand in hand.

PAT RODEGAST AND JUDITH STANTON, *EMMANUEL'S BOOK*

We must learn to stop trying to please at all costs. We must try, instead, to show the truth of ourselves, even if that means risking a 'friendship'. A true friend would prefer you to be yourself, not to pretend you're something you're not in order to please. Friendships are made from truth and love. True friends accept the truth, and they love you anyway!

Today make a conscious effort to stand by what you believe. You don't have to shout, you don't have to argue. Just be true to yourself. Respect other people's opinions, too. Respecting them does not mean you have to agree with them! Learn to show and share love regardless of your differing opinions.

Do you have a special Christmas cake? If so, prepare to ice it today. Cover the cake with either jam or marzipan to help the icing to stay on, and then follow the directions as shown on the packet of icing sugar. When you are ready to decorate the cake, rather than your usual themes, this year design an angel instead. Keep it as simple as possible or go totally lavish if you wish. Perhaps you have some little additions you can include in your design such as a bugle or star ... use your imagination and enjoy yourself!

14 December

There are hundreds of songs, hymns and carols celebrating the angels in our lives over many centuries. Choose one or more to sing today. Think of the words. Enjoy the feeling of celebration at this time as you sing to honour the gift of these angelic beings on our planet.

Love yourself, live the moment.

ANGEL INSPIRATION

Until we learn to love ourselves we cannot accept love or angels into our lives for we are putting up a barrier between us and them. Remember Jesus said, 'Love thy neighbour as you love yourself.' He was human and he knew that he must love himself first, with any faults he may have had, before he could show the same compassion to someone else. Forget yesterday, and don't be concerned about tomorrow. Yesterday is history and tomorrow is a mystery! The only way we can change the future is by our actions today. Instead of regretting the past, learn to love yourself and live this moment now, for this is the only moment that holds power.

This is the moment we can change our lives. Make a decision today to begin to love yourself and live in the 'present', this moment now.

Allow the Angel of Enthusiasm to be with you today. Enthusiasm comes from the Greek *En theo*, which means 'belief in God'. When we believe that there is a higher source, everything is possible! As it says in the Bible 'Ask and thou shalt receive.' Connect with the higher source, through your angel, today. Believe! Create today the most wonderful day of your life!

Saturnalia begins today. This is an ancient custom to honour Saturn, the Roman God of Agriculture. In those times, people hung wreaths on their doors to say they were following the Roman festival. As time wore on and Christianity grew it became a Christian and Christmas festival ritual.

This year why not expand that ritual to say 'I believe in angels!' Make or buy a picture or figure of an angel and put it on your door just as you would a Christmas wreath. (You can, of course, amalgamate the two and have a wreath with an angel.) Then, as the season unfolds, you will be able to tell just how many people in your area believe in angels!

And the angel Israfel, whose heart-strings are a lute,
and who has the sweetest voice of all God's creatures ...

THE KORAN

There is healing energy in both the singing voice and music. When did you last make music or sing? Do you immediately say you can't sing? Who told you that? Take a deep breath and begin to sing a song. Any song will do. There's certainly many you can sing which include the word 'angel' within their lyrics. What about a carol? Most people know the words, even though they may not be aware of knowing them. Go on, join in with the angels today and sing a song! If you don't have a musical instrument make one with implements from the kitchen or the office. Sing, play and laugh, and you will be that little bit closer to the angels!

One simple way to begin the healing process between yourself and someone with whom there is a problem is to write to that person's angel. (Yes, they do have one, even though it might not seem possible!)

Light a white or pink candle (white is for starting afresh, pink for unconditional love). Sit quietly and ask your own angel to guide your thoughts and your hand. Now begin the letter to that other person's angel, starting with: 'Dear Angel of .... [name]', and stating the problem. Always remember there are two sides to everything, so ask for 'the perfect outcome between me and ....'

When you are lonely, empty and afraid, remember this:
An angel who loves and cares for you is somewhere
looking for the medicine you need.
Look for the medicine messages your angel sends
you in its absence ...
in a rainbow, a dew-sparkling spider's web,
a falling feather or snowflake, or a stranger's smile ...

STEPHANIE JUNE SORRELL

As Robert Holden (author of *Laughter, the Best Medicine*) says, 'Love is the best medicine of all!' While you may feel under a tremendous amount of pressure just now as this special annual festival begins, take a few moments to show someone you love them! Make a phone call, send an email, drop by to visit. It won't cost you much more than a few minutes of your time. Isn't love worth it?

God said 'Let there be light'; and there was light.
Then heard we sounds as though the Earth did sing
And the Earth's angel cried upon the wing.

DANTE GABRIEL ROSSETTI

Today is the shortest day of the year in the Northern Hemisphere, and it is known as the Winter Solstice. (In the Southern Hemisphere, the Winter Solstice is celebrated on 21 June.) On this 'solstice' the Sun barely rises in the sky and it looks as though it is static. This is the day when we call on the angels to bring light back into our lives. The following is a simple ritual you can perform today. Try to plan it for approximately 4.15pm when the Sun begins to set. (More than likely because of the weather conditions you should do this indoors.) You will need some card-board/paper (large enough to kneel on), scissors and four candles.

Draw a large circle around you on the cardboard/paper. Make a symbol of the Sun to the east (this is the opposite direction to the setting Sun), and the symbol of the Moon to the west (the same direction as the setting Sun) on the inside of the circle, almost touching it. Place the candles at the four different directions: north/south/east/west. As you light the candles, ask the Angel Amatiel and other members of the devic kingdom to come back to the land again and bring new life to the soil.

Close your eyes and imagine the Moon lighting up the earth around you at night-time, then its place is taken by the Sun, and feel the warmth of the Sun's rays touching the soil and awakening it. Feel the Sun; know that it is returning to this place again as the weeks unfold. Imagine the Sun warming the earth. Imagine the growth underground wakening up and beginning to push towards the sunlight. Be that little seedling or bulb in your mind's eye. Unfold from hibernation and begin to seek the light above you. Know that there is a path to follow, there is light at the end of the struggle. Allow your heart to fill with joy as you finally push through to the light! Let the candles burn themselves out.

Today the Sun moves into the Earth sign of Capricorn, which is looked after by Archangel Michael. Capricorn is named after the goat. The positive traits of this sign are hard work, commitment, family-oriented energies; the negative side is low self-esteem and 'scapegoat' or victim-consciousness. Archangel Michael can be called into your life today and any day during the next four weeks (regardless of your zodiac sign) to help you to face what needs to be faced and make the right choices for your future. This Archangel is seen as the protector, but we must also be willing to make decisions ourselves.

Light an orange or gold candle today and invite Archangel Michael to be with you and those you love for the coming month ahead.

The Christmas season can be so demanding on our time, our patience and our pocket! It's easy to lose sight of our priorities with so much going on about us. No matter how rushed you feel today give yourself at least five minutes to sit down and breathe deeply and relax. The more you breathe in this way, the easier you will handle stress. Now that you are sitting down, write out a list of all the talents and special gifts you have been given. Continue by adding family support, friendships, and angels of course! How much would you have to spend to have so much in your life? These gifts are priceless. Don't throw them away!

In Ireland and the UK we hang up a stocking at the chimney of our home for Santa Claus to fill with goodies. This ritual goes back to Celtic times when the people believed that all good things come down from the skies, and that they come down in a funnel of light from above. The chimney is like a funnel, bringing energy down from Heaven. Where else, if you are awaiting good things to come from Heaven, would you put your stocking, but beside the chimney?

Whatever your circumstances, invite the Angel of Divine Goodness to come into your life today so that you can share joy, friendship and love with those around you.

25 December

Celebrate this day! (Concern yourself only with today.)

ANGEL INSPIRATION

Take a deep breath and, as you breathe in, breathe in the energy of trust. Trust that all is well, that you will be looked after. Now breathe out any fears. Today is a day for celebration, no matter what your religion or your culture. Learn to celebrate today: celebrate the fact that you are alive, that you are breathing, that you have friends, family, angels and spirit guides in your life. Concern yourself only with trust and love today. By your actions today you can ensure that the future will be brighter and better for you.

Make a pendulum with a clear quartz crystal or a piece of wood or resin and a chain or thread or string. Ask your angel to help you to receive the answers to your questions.

Hold the pendulum loosely in your hand from the top of the chain or thread. Close your eyes and ask the angels to help the pendulum move in the direction of 'Yes'. Allow the pendulum to move and then open your eyes and note if it's clockwise, anti-clockwise or up and down. Stop it, then again close your eyes and ask your angel for the pendulum's 'No' answer. Again wait for it to move and then open your eyes and note its direction. (If it stays static that in itself is the answer.) Now devise some questions you can ask about the year ahead. Note you can only ask for a 'yes' or 'no'. As you get each answer, ask another more pertinent question, something like 'Should I change my career next year?' If the answer is 'yes' then ask something more pertinent such as 'Should I go back to college?' If the answer is 'yes' ask 'Should I choose veterinary college?' or some similar specific question. If you get stuck, ask your angel for more guidance!

If you've indulged in turkey and ham over the last few days you're sure to enjoy this simple and quick pasta dish, **Red-haired Angel Pasta**.

To serve four people, you will need:
    450 g/ 1 lb angel hair pasta
    100 g/ 4oz of sundried tomatoes in oil
    oil from sundried tomatoes or 2 tablespoons olive oil
    black pepper
    Parmesan cheese

Boil the pasta until it has reached the 'al dente' stage, then drain. Meanwhile, cut up the sundried tomatoes into small pieces. Fry them quickly in their own oil if possible (if not, olive oil) for about 2 minutes, to ensure they are heated through. Then add the pasta to the tomatoes. Add black pepper. Stir quickly so that the tomatoes and pepper are coating the pasta, then serve. Sprinkle with Parmesan cheese, as required.

28 December

Humans must be known to be loved.
Angels must be loved to be known.

ANON

We don't have to have educational degrees, professorships or other academic titles in order to be in touch with angels. It is only by opening up our hearts to our angels that we can connect with them. Sit quietly today and open up your heart. Imagine your angel is sitting opposite you right now. Close your eyes, breathe in deeply and imagine your angel's golden light of love is filling your heart. With every out-breath you are releasing fear and judgement. With every in-breath you are accepting angelic love. Enjoy the sensation! Practise it for a few moments every day and see how your world will change!

You don't want to take 'baggage' with you into the new calendar year, so get ready now to clear away, once and for all, any unforgiveness or resentment you may be feeling about people in the past.

This is a very simple, but powerful, ritual. Do this when you are alone and think about each person clearly, in as much detail as possible, then say their name out loud and:

'I forgive you for not being as I wanted you to be. I forgive you and I set you free.'

By saying this, you are now freeing yourself from the lesson you needed to learn with them.

Have you been keeping up your Angel Journal that you began at the beginning of the year? If you have, it's a good time to go through it now as we come to the end of the calendar year.

How has your angel helped you to face change in your life? How often have you been aware that your angel is beside you, guiding you along?

If you've been following the daily suggestions in this book you should be very aware of and feel very close to your beloved friend.

What would you like for the world in general in the year ahead? Call on the Angel of Divine Peace to come into your life today and stay for evermore. As you know, peace must start within each of us before it can grow into a world-wide energy. By radiating peace outwards to your loved ones, your neighbours, your environment, you will begin a world-wide energy flow that cannot be stopped!

Light some incense and a candle to thank the Angel of December, Hanael, for being in your life this month. December is a month for finding balance between giving and receiving, activity and relaxation. Did you learn to prioritise with Angel Hanael's help? Did you discover and acknowledge your own special gifts and talents? Whether you used this book regularly or just dipped in, did you feel yourself becoming closer to your angel? Now on this, the last day of the calendar year, sit quietly, play some gentle music, imagine your own angel is right in front of you and ...

... open your heart to angel love.

ANGEL INSPIRATION

About the Author

If you have enjoyed this book you may wish to know that the following items are also available from Margaret Neylon at the address below.

Guided visualizations on cassette as follows:
Talking with Angels, Healing with Angels, Angel Love and Angel Magic

Angel Inspiration Cards (set of 40 'angelic messages')

Margaret Neylon is available to give workshops, and can be contacted at:

'Angelgate'   Or you can contact her directly
Virginia   by email:
County Cavan   **angelgate@eircom.net**
Ireland

By the same author
Angel Magic

*Thanks so much to everyone who has given me
so much support in my work, and especially
Jo, my inspirational editor!*